For years the public has been waiting for a truly fine handbook of drawing and painting that would help the student and the week-end painter alike to grasp the principles of their chosen medium and apply them directly to the problems they face in the studio, the classroom and on field·trips.

HOW TO DRAW AND PAINT

is just such a book. It treats in detail the entire range of major painting media. The list of subjects on the back cover of this volume gives only a hint of the ground covered.

Page-for-page this is the outstanding book of its kind available today— and so handy you can take it with you wherever you go.

HOW

DRAW

TO
AND PAINT

BY HENRY GASSER, N.A.

A DELL FIRST EDITION

Published by
DELL PUBLISHING·CO., INC.
750 Third Avenue
New York 17, N.Y.

Library of Congress Catalog Card No. 55-11192

B-107
Previous Dell editions #FE54
    and #LC125

New Dell edition:

First printing—October, 1958
Second printing—October, 1959
Third printing—July, 1960
Fourth printing—August, 1961
Fifth printing—October, 1962
Sixth printing—November, 1963

Printed in U.S.A.

ABOUT THE AUTHOR

Henry Gasser, N.A. studied at the Newark School of Fine and Industrial Art, the Grand Central School of Art and the Art Students' League.

His paintings have been exhibited throughout the United States and abroad, winning a number of important awards. He is represented in over twenty-six museum collections including the Boston, Philadelphia and Newark museums.

Mr. Gasser has lectured and demonstrated painting techniques for art groups and schools throughout the country. From 1946-1954 he was Director of the Newark School of Fine and Industrial Art.

He is a member of over fifteen art societies including the National Academy, the American Watercolor Society, Philadelphia Watercolor Club, New Jersey Watercolor Society, Audubon Artists, Salmagundi Club and the National Arts Club.

Mr. Gasser is the author of OIL PAINTING: METHODS AND DEMONSTRATIONS (Reinhold); CASEIN PAINTING: METHODS AND DEMONSTRATIONS (Watson Guptill); and WATERCOLOR: HOW TO DO IT.

HOW TO
DRAW AND PAINT

INTRODUCTION

"Do it yourself!" Every day new thousands of Americans, men and women alike, are discovering the fun, the deep and lasting satisfaction they can derive from making things themselves, with their own hands.

This book is addressed to the aristocrat of all "do-it-yourselfers"—to you, the beginning artist. Whatever your goal in art—whether you hope to become another Rembrandt, a top-flight commercial artist, or just a happy amateur—*How to Draw and Paint* should help smooth the way for you.

As teacher and art school director, I have been in a position to observe the development of several thousand students. The great majority worked hard, and were fortunate in that they were obtaining instruction from an able faculty. Many amateurs labor diligently too, but most of them do not have the advantage of professional guidance. Consequently they unknowingly repeat their mistakes and, in general, do things the hard way.

Now, a book cannot, of course, take the place of an art school or a teacher, but certainly it can serve as an approach to painting. *How to Draw and Paint* contains information on drawing and sketching, characteristics of paints, preparations for painting, step-by-step demonstrations in all media, technical recipes, and general guidance in picture-making. All that and much more you will find—and, I trust, find helpful—in the pages that follow.

The step-by-step demonstrations, which I use to show

how particular subjects can be developed, should not be regarded as hard-and-fast formulae. Each demonstration is but one of many possible ways to approach and depict the subject. It is up to you to experiment and thus to discover the best way to express yourself.

There is no easy way to learn to paint well ("Art is long," remember), but if this book at least *helps* you to follow in the footsteps of successful artists, then its purpose will have been achieved.

OIL PAINTING

AN INTRODUCTION TO OIL PAINTING

Oil painting is the ideal medium for the novice. It is an excellent way to study, because changes and corrections are easily made. Unwanted passages of color can be scraped off the canvas any number of times without injury to the surface. One color can be painted over another, drawing and proportions can be corrected, and all the nuances of light and shadow can be studied experimentally. The painting can be put aside at any time, to be picked up and continued at a later date.

Some beginners choose oil without considering other media because of a reverence for the "genuine oil painting." When they take up painting as a hobby they want to produce "pictures that show the actual brush strokes." Many other amateurs, who would like to work in several media but feel that their time is too limited, select oil after checking with teachers or schools or experimenting on their own. Even a person who is more interested in another medium may find, as I have, that by using oils he can more easily study color subtleties and can acquire basic knowledge that will later be applied to the medium he prefers. The old adage, "One medium helps another," is especially true if the first one is oil.

As you progress you will soon discover that there is more to oil painting than the surface quality of the brush work. The type of surface you work on, the preliminary staining of the surface, and the underpainting all affect the finished result.

However, in your initial efforts you will want to work in a direct manner, particularly when painting outdoors. Later you can experiment in the studio with various types of underpainting.

MATERIAL AND EQUIPMENT
FOR OIL PAINTING

Colors

If you are just beginning to paint, you will do well to start with a reputable brand of student color. Most color manufacturers make a line of student colors along with their professional grades. These colors are appreciably less expensive and the selection is nearly as wide as in the professional line. As you progress, you can replace the student brand with colors of professional quality, which have far greater covering quality, particularly in the Cadmiums and Blues. There are several good brands of colors available. My own choice is the Grumbacher line.

I recommend the following colors for basic use:

> *Alizarin Crimson*
> *Cadmium Yellow, Light*
> *Cadmium Red, Light*
> *French Ultramarine*
> *Ivory Black*
> *Light Red*
> *Thalo Green*
> *Yellow Ochre*
> *Zinc or Titanium White*

These nine colors will enable you to mix the various shades of other colors that you will need for most purposes.

14

However, you may want to supplement these colors with:

Cadmium Yellow, Deep ✓
Cadmium Orange
Cerulean Blue ✓
Burnt Sienna
Viridian
Cobalt Blue ✓
Thalo Blue ✓
Raw Umber ✓

In the study of Color, page 32, the handling of these colors is described in detail.

Canvas and Other Painting Surfaces

The best and most receptive surface on which to work is stretched linen canvas. Linen, however, is relatively expensive, and cotton canvas is a good substitute. The cotton canvas panels that fit in your paint box are the most convenient for painting outdoors and are inexpensive. They are light in weight, too, and have the added advantage of not taking up much space when stored in your studio.

The chief disadvantage of any type of panel is its lack of resiliency. Stretched canvas, whether cotton or linen, has a drum-like quality that seems to add vigor to your brush stroke. It also has the advantage of being available in several types of surfaces, from extra-smooth (double-primed) to very rough. You will find a medium-rough texture best for all-around work; extra-smooth is generally used for portraits.

These various textures are not available in canvas panels; when a panel is made, its adherence to the board flattens out the texture. I suggest that you use panels when working outdoors and stretched canvas when developing your painting indoors.

You may want to make your own panels. Today many artists use Masonite, which can be bought at any lumber supply house. While several thicknesses are available, the 1/8 inch is the least expensive and can safely be used in any size up to 24 x 30 inches. Masonite has a rough and a smooth side; both surfaces are usable, but the rough side gives an uninteresting and monotonous texture to the finished painting and also requires much more paint to cover the surface. Use the smooth side for outdoor work, when speed is necessary to capture a changing scene.

Whichever surface will be used should first be rubbed with sandpaper, then a coat of flake white should be brushed on. When the first coat is dry, give the panel another coat if the brown undertone of the masonite shows through. The panel is ready for use as soon as the final coat of white lead is dry to the touch. It will save time to have the lumber house cut a number of boards to the required size; then you can coat all of them at once.

Besides canvas and Masonite, there are various synthetic painting boards on the market. Since they are substitutes for real canvas, they cost less and are not as durable.

Painters can even make their own panels with a good quality chip board, a heavy gray cardboard. Chip board will last better if it is given a coat or two of shellac to reduce its natural absorbency, and a coating of flake white over that will create a more receptive surface. Covering the back as well as the edges with shellac will seal the panel against moisture and add somewhat to its durability.

Making Your Own Canvas Panels

You can also make your own canvas panels. The most economical way is to purchase a roll of either cotton or linen canvas, in a width that will not waste canvas when it is cut up. For example, a 50-inch width will give you two 20-x-24-inch panels. It is not advisable to make panels any larger than this size, since larger ones may warp.

Get some beaverboard—extra heavy cardboard known as mounting board—and cut to the desired size. Cut the canvas about ½ inch larger all around than the size of the board. Apply glue to the back of the entire canvas and mount on the board. After trimming the corners, fold over the surplus ½-inch margin. Place the mounted canvas on the floor and put a drawing board on it, making certain that it covers the entire canvas. Place several heavy books on top of the drawing board and allow to press overnight. Then cut a sheet of heavy brown wrapping paper to a size slightly less than the mounted canvas. Glue this paper to the back of the panel and repeat the pressing process. This acts as a counter-mount and prevents warping. I suggest that you experiment first with pieces of scrap canvas, then if you find this method satisfactory you will want to do several panels at one time. The process is such that it is almost as easy to mount a half dozen panels as to mount one.

Stretching Your Own Canvas

You can purchase canvas already stretched if you work in the stock sizes (8 x 10, 9 x 12, 12 x 16, 16 x 20, 20 x 24, and 24 x 30 inches). If you want a special size, or prefer to do your own stretching, the process is fairly simple. You will need canvas pliers, which can be obtained in any art sup-

ply shop, stretcher strips of the size desired, and a box of
⅜-inch tacks. We will assume that you want to stretch a
20-x-24-inch canvas. Cut a piece of canvas 22 x 26 inches,
which will give you a working edge of 1 inch all around the
stretcher strips. The strips are placed in a frame position,
as square as possible. Place the canvas so that the even
1-inch margin appears around the stretcher frame. Hammer a tack partly in the center of each of the four sides.
Then, gripping the 1-inch edge with the pliers, hammer
a tack on each side of the center (about 2 inches apart). Repeat this procedure until all four sides have three tacks.
Then keep adding more tacks, working from the center
toward the corners, alternately on each side. Gradually
the canvas will be tacked along the side of the entire frame.
Until you get the knack of exactly how hard to pull the
canvas with the pliers, just hammer the tacks in lightly.
Then if you should get any unwanted wrinkles you can
easily remove the tacks, tighten the wrinkled area, and
retack. The wedges that come with the wooden stretchers
can then be hammered into the corners to take up the
slack.

The Paint Box and Palette

You will need a box to store your colors as well as to
hold brushes, palette, and panels when you go sketching.

The most popular sizes for paint boxes are 12 x 16 and
16 x 20 inches; the box lid should be grooved to hold canvas panels of the same size. A box in either of these sizes will
serve both for the studio and outdoors. Paint boxes are
available in wood and metal. Metal ones are more expensive but will last a lifetime, and wooden ones already
painted or stained cost more than unpainted ones. If you
buy an unfinished box, give it a complete coat of good
varnish, both inside and out. It is easier to wipe off any

unwanted paint on a varnished surface, and the varnish will also help to preserve the wood. For any wooden box, check the hardware, making certain that the hinges and clasps are substantial, and check the lid to be sure it will hold the panels comfortably. Inexpensive boxes occasionally warp, making it difficult to slide the panels in the slots of the lid.

You can buy a paint box completely outfitted with tubes of color. If the assortment happens to be made up of the colors you want, that is fine, but some dealers stock their boxes with colors that are seldom used. If this should be the case, by all means purchase the empty box and select only the colors you want to use, rather than confuse your palette with unnecessary colors.

A wooden palette fitted to the paint box is generally supplied. Give it a coating of linseed oil before using it. Remove the surplus paint from your palette at the end of each day's work, then rub it well with a paint rag, using linseed oil occasionally. In time your palette will acquire a beautiful protective sheen and will give you an excellent surface for mixing colors.

The Easel and Other Equipment

There are two main types of easels, studio and outdoor or sketching easels. If you purchase a sketching easel, select one that folds into a small, compact unit. Remember that you will be carrying a paint box and probably a sketching stool along with the easel.

A sketching easel can be used for working indoors, but it will lack the stability of a regular studio easel and will limit the size of your canvas, because the grips on a sketching easel are not designed to hold large canvases. Its stability can be improved by placing rubber tips on its legs when it is used indoors.

Whatever easel you select, make certain that it contains a fixture that allows the canvas to be tilted at an angle to eliminate surface glare.

The Palette Knife

You will need a palette knife for removing paint from your palette as you work. It can also be used to scrape unwanted paint from the surface of the canvas before repainting, and it can supplement a brush in mixing colors.

Medium

A painting medium, or vehicle, is necessary to make the paint workable. I recommend that you buy a prepared copal painting medium and use it at the start. Later on, you may want to prepare your own medium. A good homemade mixture is one-third turpentine, one-third linseed oil, and one-third copal oil varnish. You can vary the effect by using more turpentine in the preliminary stages of a painting, to speed the drying as well as to thin the consistency of the paint. Then, as the painting builds up, cut down on the turpentine and use more linseed oil, painting in a heavier manner.

When you are more experienced, you may want to experiment with other painting mediums. Stand oil, which gives an enamel-like finish to a painting, is a very heavy oil and should be thinned with turpentine to make it workable. Sun-thickened oil will also add a gloss to your painting and it dries faster than stand oil.

All mediums should be purchased at an art supply shop to insure high quality.

Retouch Varnish

It will not be necessary to carry a bottle of retouch

varnish in your paint box, but you should have it on hand in the studio. When a canvas is worked on over a period of time, some color areas go dull as they dry, and brushing or spraying some retouch varnish over the painting brightens the sunken colors. Retouch varnish also helps the adherence of the paint film of subsequent work. Do not overuse this varnish; it will not be needed until the painting is well under way.

Oil Cups

You should have two cups that can be fastened to your palette. One cup is for the medium you are mixing with your colors, the other holds turpentine for cleaning your brush quickly, particularly when working outdoors. Make sure both cups are big enough to take a large brush.

Charcoal Pencils

Always have some fairly soft charcoal pencils or sticks in your paint box. Charcoal allows more flexible handling than an ordinary lead pencil in making the basic sketch on the canvas.

Fixatif

A fixatif is used to keep the charcoal drawing from smudging; it is sprayed on with a small atomizer. This can be omitted when the sketching is done outdoors, and the surplus charcoal can be dusted off the canvas with a rag or a chamois. Dust lightly so that a faint image remains to guide you in the later painting.

Paint Rags

Have enough rags in your paint box for wiping your brushes and palette, and for general cleaning up.

The Sketching Stool

If you prefer to sit while working, you will need a sketching stool. Choose one that is light in weight but sturdily constructed and that will fold up and use as little space as possible when you are carrying the rest of your sketching material. Some painters dispense with an easel and instead carry a second stool, on which they set the open paint box with a panel inserted in the lid.

Brushes

Bristle brushes are the most popular brushes for oil painting. The most commonly used types are the long-haired brush—known as a "flat"—and the short-haired brush—a "bright." There is also a round bristle brush that comes to a blunt point, which you may find useful after you have become familiar with the possibilities of the long- and short-haired varieties. These come in sizes from a scant 1/8 inch to over 1 inch in width and are identified by numbers.

While I suggest inexpensive student colors for beginners, I recommend that you buy the best brushes you can afford. Properly cared for, a good brush will hold its shape and resiliency and will last a long time. In Brush Handling, page 26, advice is given on the care of brushes and the use of other types of brushes.

The following sizes should enable you to accomplish all the work necessary on canvases from 9 x 12 to 20 x 24 inches:

> Long-haired brushes numbers 2, 4, 6, and 8
> Short-haired brushes numbers 4 and 6

In addition to the bristle brushes, you may find a small pointed or round sable brush handy for fine lines and details.

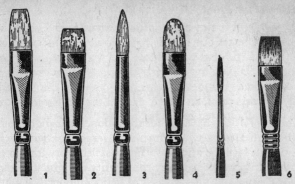

BRUSHES courtesy of M. Grumbacher, Inc., Mfr. of Brushes, Colors, Artists' Material

No. 1   Flat
The long-haired bristle brush known as a "flat." It will serve for the bulk of your work.

No. 2   Bright
Also a bristle brush but with a shorter hair. Using the edge of the brush produces a thin line, excellent for outlining.

No. 3   Round
The round brush is available in both bristle and sable hair. It does not hold much paint but is useful for details.

No. 4   Filbert
Combines the characteristics of a flat and a round bristle brush. A very fluent stroke, particularly useful for head and figure painting, can be produced with it.

No. 5   Rigger
Made with sable hair, the rigger is used for delineating fine lines and sharp details.

No. 6   Flat Sable
The flat sable is the most effective brush for producing a smooth finish. Its soft quality lends itself well to glazing effects.

THE HOME STUDIO

Not all of us can have the ideal studio with skylight and north light. However, a room with average-size windows that do not face the afternoon sun is satisfactory for most painters. In portrait painting the quality of light striking both the sitter and the canvas is of major importance, but for other work the light problem is less acute. A white ceiling and neutral gray walls will help when working with color in either natural or artificial light. It is important to avoid disturbing shadows and strong reflected light.

Working under artificial light has always been a problem, but today's fluorescent lamps give a fair approximation of daylight. If you find such lighting a bit on the cool side, supplement it with the light from an ordinary incandescent bulb. I find that a blend of the two crossing my working area is most satisfactory. For mixing colors it is important that the source of light be of the same quality as that for the surface upon which you are working.

A daylight bulb can be substituted for the fluorescent lamp. Since it too has a bluish cast, an ordinary incandescent bulb should also be added to it.

A taboret or small table placed close to the easel is a good idea. Many artists, with the exception of portrait painters, have given up constantly holding their palette while working. Instead, they rest it on a table of convenient height close to the canvas.

An extra table for setting up a still-life subject and for general utility use should complete your immediate needs.

CARE OF EQUIPMENT

• Clean all brushes thoroughly at the end of the day's work.

• Make certain that you replace the cap of each color tube immediately after using it.

• Do not allow the oil in the palette cup to accumulate and become gummy.

• Remove unwanted paint from the working surface of the palette knife, then wipe the palette clean with a rag.

• Wipe the palette knife frequently, never allowing the paint to become tacky on the blade.

• Take care not to nick the blade of the palette knife.

• Before folding up an outdoor easel, always remove any paint that may have smeared on it. Check especially the cross-piece that supports the canvas.

• Keep a small pair of pliers in your paint box for use in removing caps, when they stick to the tube. If a cap does not unscrew, light a match and hold the flame at the cap. The heat should soften any dried paint, which is generally the cause of the sticking.

• Although most paint boxes are sold with a protective coating on the outside, many manufacturers leave the inside untouched. A few coats of shellac will help to preserve the wood and will make paint smears easier to remove.

• Never store materials or equipment in a damp place. This applies particularly to paper and canvas.

BRUSH HANDLING

In an earlier section I listed the essential brushes needed for painting (see page 22), but as you progress you will naturally want to add to your collection. As you paint more you will realize the importance of good brushes, too. A good brush will hold its shape and, with good care, will last several years, but an inferior brush never has the spring and resiliency of a more expensive make. Inferior brushes also have the infuriating habit of depositing loose hairs on the painted canvas. This always seems to happen when you have just executed a particularly fine color passage!

Start to paint by dipping the brush lightly into the color, taking care not to let the color come up to the ferrule. Use the rag frequently, removing surplus color and at the same time pressing the hairs back into shape. If you lay-in your paintings in a dry-brush manner, that is, applying color with a rubbing technique and with little or no medium, use one of your older stiff bristle brushes. Once you start using full color, apply it with a crisp, firm touch.

You can clean your brush fairly well while working by dipping it into the turpentine and wiping it dry with a rag. However, when a deep blue or violet color is followed with a shade of yellow, the darker color may tint the lighter one in spite of the quick turpentine rinse. You will find it convenient, therefore, to use a separate brush for lighter colors, particularly the yellows and ochre. Many painters use several brushes when working outdoors, reserving a brush for yellows, one for blues, another for reds, and so on. That may not always be necessary, but it is advisable to have separate brushes for Thalo colors, whose tinting quality is so powerful that they can easily find their way into all the colors used.

Use as large a brush as possible for the area to be covered. This will insure a broad style. Bristle brushes are preferable to sable brushes for most of your paintings, because they impart a more vital stroke to the canvas. Using a sable brush at too early a stage of the painting can lead to an undesirable slickness.

Oil brushes are made with long handles for a purpose. Much painting is accomplished by holding the end of the brush handle—particularly in the early stages of a canvas. This enables you to paint with more freedom and, since you are holding the brush at arm's length, to see your work more clearly. Then, as the canvas becomes covered with color, details can be added by grasping the brush by its metal ferrule.

Holding the brush like a pencil is almost instinctive, but you should experiment with the effects that are achieved by handling the brush in various other ways. Notice how the color is deposited on the canvas when you pull the brush firmly downward, in contrast to holding it lightly and patting the color on gently. Try painting a thin line by twirling a pointed brush between your forefinger and thumb; the resulting line will be broken and softer than when the brush is gripped by the ferrule. Keep this in mind for rendering tree branches without leaves, wires, ropes, and similar lines. As you work you will find that long-haired bristle brushes produce a more fluid stroke than short-haired brushes. The flat sable brush with its soft hair will be found useful for smoothing rough passages, blending various colors together, and generally refining the painting.

Give your much used brushes a rest every so often. After washing them thoroughly, place the brush part between the pages of a heavy book for a few days. This will help to hold their shape and add to their life.

In addition to turpentine, which is convenient for cleaning brushes quickly while painting, soap and water should be used regularly. Use a mild soap and lukewarm water. Work up a lather with the soap and rub the lather well into the brushes. Pay special attention to cleaning the brush where it meets the ferrule. It is when the paint becomes imbedded into this area that the brush loses its shape. Rinse thoroughly with the lukewarm water, making certain that all the soap is removed. Finish rinsing with cold water. Then, with your thumb and forefinger, squeeze the surplus water out, and at the same time reshape the brush. Put clean brushes in an upright container, brush end up.

Do not discard old brushes; you will find them useful for achieving certain effects that can be obtained only with a worn brush. I have some brushes in my collection that have just a few wisps of hair remaining, but I still find use for them.

If you accidentally allow the color to dry in a brush, try soaking it in turpentine or kerosene overnight. If the color still adheres, use a commercial paint remover as a last resort. No brush is ever quite the same again after the powerful remover is used, so make every attempt not to allow the color to set in your brushes.

There is an excellent brush- and hand-cleaning fluid on the market. The cleaning agent is properly balanced and will not harm brushes. Color is removed faster with less rubbing, and the fluid acts to preserve the brush.

A brush that has lost its shape can be restored to some degree by being dipped in a mild solution of mucilage and water. First properly shape the brush hairs with the fingers. The mucilage will hold the hairs in position. Allow the solution to remain on overnight, then soak the brush in warm water to remove the mucilage. The brush will generally come back to a semblance of its original shape.

Sketch At All Times

ARRANGING THE COLORS
ON THE PALETTE

The purpose of arranging the colors on your palette in a systematic way is to save time. There should be no fumbling around to find a color, for all your attention should be concentrated on painting the subject before you.

If the colors are always kept in the same order on your palette, your brush will instinctively go to the desired color.

There are several ways of setting up a palette. The colors can be arranged from warm to cool or vice-versa. They can be placed just along the far edge of the palette or form an inverted L by also being placed along the left edge. The oil cups—one for the painting medium, the other for turpentine—can be fastened to the right side by themselves, so that they are quickly accessible.

Do not skimp on the color you squeeze from a tube. Too small an amount of each color on the palette leads to thin painting. If you paint on consecutive days, most of the paint will remain workable. If any color starts drying out, scrape it off with the palette knife and replace it with fresh color.

Unused color can be placed in a dish and covered with water, which will keep it fresh for several days. When you are ready to re-use it, pour the water from the dish and transfer the paint back to the palette with a knife. Any layer of skin that may have formed can easily be removed and the paint will be workable again.

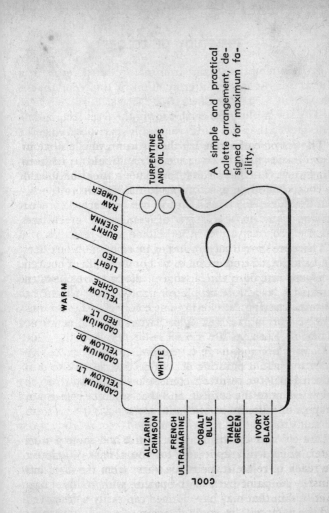

A simple and practical palette arrangement, designed for maximum facility.

WARM

RAW UMBER
BURNT SIENNA
LIGHT RED
YELLOW OCHRE
CADMIUM RED LT.
CADMIUM YELLOW DP
CADMIUM YELLOW LT.

TURPENTINE AND OIL CUPS

WHITE

ALIZARIN CRIMSON
FRENCH ULTRAMARINE
COBALT BLUE
THALO GREEN
IVORY BLACK

COOL

THE STUDY OF COLOR

Early attempts to paint from nature often result in a literal, almost crude, interpretation of the color that is seen.

The sky is blue, the earth brown, the trees seem a definite green. It is not until you really start observing the subtleties of color that you begin to avoid the obvious. You discover that the sky can vary from light gray to greenish brown. The brown earth becomes a pinkish violet or even a vivid orange, according to the light from the sky. Subtle blues, violets, and browns can be detected in what first appeared to be a cluster of monotonous green trees. As you progress you learn to become more selective. You emphasize colors that produce a more harmonious effect and subdue discordant notes or eliminate them entirely.

If you were born with a sense of color you are one of the fortunate few. Most people constantly have to return to nature, studying the effect of one color related to another, always working to seek color harmonies and new color schemes. Then, as the eye for color develops, the painter's work becomes more distinctive.

In the actual painting of a subject we learn that a restricted palette insures better color harmony, that the grays enhance the subject, and that restraint is necessary when using the more brilliant colors.

Study the original paintings or good color reproductions of the old and modern masters. Notice how some painters actually used very few colors, yet you are not conscious of any lack of color in their paintings; others seem to have run the gamut of every color, but they also produced beautiful harmonies.

You may want to study the scientific color theories of the authorities on the subject. Many books are available,

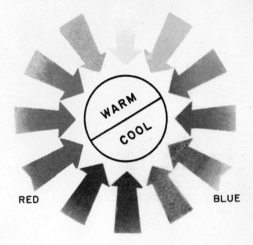

RED   BLUE

Color Wheel courtesy of M. Grumbacher, Inc.
Brushes ● Colors ● Artists' Material

but before you become too involved with theory remember that you are interested not only in the visual effect of color and its emotional impact, but also in how color creates form and how form is affected by its surrounding color.

Technically, any color can be made by mixing the primary colors, yellow, red, and blue. Each of the secondary colors, orange, violet, and green, is made by mixing the two primary colors on either side of it.

Mixing primary and secondary colors produces the intermediate colors, yellow-orange, red-orange, red-violet, blue-violet, blue-green, and yellow-green.

The complement of each color is directly opposite it. Mixtures of complements make grays.

Colors containing a greater proportion of yellow or red are considered "warm." Conversely, colors containing a greater proportion of blue are "cool."

Color Mixing

A. The three primary colors, yellow, red, and blue, mixed together neutralize each other to make a gray.

B. The three secondary colors, orange, violet, and green, mixed together neutralize each other to make a gray.

C. Two primary colors, in this case yellow and red, mixed together make a secondary color (orange).

D. Two primary colors, in this case blue and yellow, mixed together make a secondary color (green).

E. A primary color (yellow) mixed with a secondary color (green) makes an intermediate hue (yellow-green).

F. Two primary colors, in this case red and blue, mixed together make a secondary color (violet).

G. Two colors opposite each other on the color wheel (complementary colors) mixed together neutralize each other to make a gray. In this case yellow and violet were mixed to produce a gray.

H. When black is mixed with a color, it grays the color to produce a neutralized hue. In this case black was added to red to make a neutralized red.

I. When a neutralized color is mixed with a color, it grays the color to produce a neutralized hue. In this case a deep brown was added to blue to make a neutralized blue.

J. Here is another neutralized color mixed with a color to produce a neutralized hue. In this case a reddish brown was added to violet to make a neutralized violet.

Color mixing is generally the first stumbling block for the novice. His first attempts result in either a pale, thin, washed-out painting or a heavy, muddy effect. In the first instance, too little color is mixed with too much white paint and these mixtures are applied too timidly.

Keep the use of white paint to a minimum. Rather,

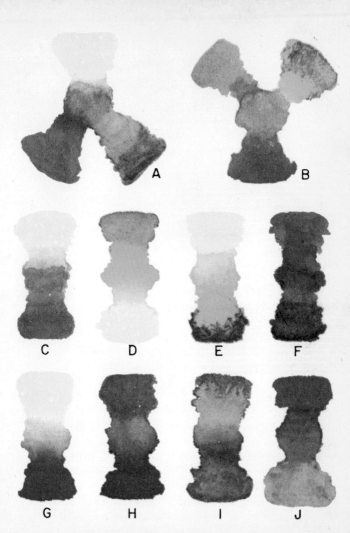

A

B

C D E F

G H I J

exaggerate the color you see in the subject when transferring it to the canvas. It is easier to modify it with white paint later, when the canvas is covered and you compare it with the subject. Chances are the color will not be as strong as you had thought and will require little or no changing. White paint is best used sparingly with each color. For example, to get a secondary color like a light green we know that the primary colors to be used are blue and yellow. Rather than mixing these two colors together and then adding white, cut each color first with white and then mix them. A far more vibrant secondary color results. This is particularly true when mixing violet. Many students get a muddy-looking violet when mixing red and blue together and then adding white. If the resulting color is too light, they add blue. It then turns out to be too cool so red is put into the mixture. By this time the color has become too dark and more white is needed, and in all probability the mixture then has to be discarded and a fresh start made.

The thinness of the paint layer is frequently caused by the use of too much medium, especially turpentine.

A heavy, muddy-looking canvas is usually the result of mixing too many colors together in striving to capture the desired effect. Learn to know all the possibilities of the colors you are using on your palette. Work first with fewer colors—you will be astounded at the many shades that can be produced with only a few colors.

You will also find it valuable to experiment with making a color darker or grayer by combining it with its opposite instead of the obvious black. Black has a place in the mixing of color, but use it sparingly until you have learned the possibilities of the primary and secondary colors.

It is fumbling in mixing colors and applying them to canvas, then repainting the same area in an attempt to correct the color, that contributes to a heavy, over-painted picture.

Do not become discouraged when your early attempts to mix colors correctly produce any of these unhappy results. The technique of color mixing is always acquired gradually. Later on you will obtain the desired color by using much less paint than you do now. You will mix two colors, possibly modify them with a touch of a third color, or even deepen the hue with a dab of a fourth color.

Avoid stirring paint mixtures too much on the palette. Mixing colors on the canvas will create a more lively and sparkling effect.

Color-Mixing Exercises

Before working with the full range of your palette, you should familiarize yourself with the possibilities of each color.

An excellent start is to take a warm and a cool color and do a complete painting limiting yourself to these two colors. A good combination is Cobalt Blue and Burnt Sienna or French Ultramarine and Burnt Umber. You can use water color or oil; for the latter, white paint must be added. Improvise a landscape or build one from an outdoor sketch that you may have on hand. With blue as the cool color and brown as the warm, begin to paint the picture.

In some areas you will use the colors pure; in others, they will be combined. You will be amazed at the number of color variations that can be achieved with so simple a palette. Most important, you will discover the numerous shades of warm and cool grays that are obtainable.

For the next exercise, use three colors and explore their possibilities. Cobalt Blue, Light Red, and Yellow Ochre should allow you plenty of scope compared to the two-color exercise. Again, add white paint if you use oils. By painting the same subject used before, you will more readily realize the added possibilities of a third color.

Experiment along these lines by making up your own limited color combinations. Add a fourth color, and so on, until you acquire a working knowledge of all the colors you plan to use on your palette.

One important point will become apparent: The fewer colors you use, the easier it is to obtain color harmony. Every time a new color is added the risk of creating discord is increased.

Color-Mixing Hints

• Restrict your mixtures to as few colors as possible.
• Yellow is the most sensitive color on the palette. Use a knife to scoop it up when mixing it with other colors. Daubing a brush that you have been using into the yellow may stain it.
• Take care when using white paint. Keep in mind that it neutralizes the color with which it is mixed. Too much white will impart a washed-out or chalky look to the color mixture.
• Mix colors with the tip of the brush hairs. Never allow the paint to seep up to the metal ferrule.
• Keep two jars of water handy when mixing water color. If you use one to rinse color from your brush the other will remain clear for a longer time, thus assuring clean water for mixing.
• Dipping a brush into two colors and not stirring the mixture on the palette but applying it directly to the canvas often produces an interesting broken-color effect. This can be done with water color as well, but a minimum amount of water must be used. Warm and cool contrasting colors

are most effective.

• If you paint flowers or portraits you may have to add extra colors to your palette, because certain shades needed in such work are almost impossible to mix with a standard color palette.

Permanence of Colors

You should learn the permanence of your colors as soon as possible. Today's manufacturers have overcome many defects in both the mixing and the lasting qualities of paints, and many colors that for years were listed as non-permanent or doubtful have either been eliminated or, through modern methods, made permanent.

Here is a list of colors that most color manufacturers consider permanent (these apply to all media):

Alizarin Crimson
Burnt Sienna
Burnt Umber
Cadmium colors (all)
Cerulean Blue
Chromium Oxide Green (opaque)
Cobalt Blue, Light and Deep
Cobalt Violet
Flesh
Grumbacher Red
Indian Red
Ivory Black
Lamp Black
Lemon Yellow (Hansa Yellow)
Light Red (English Red)
Manganese Blue
Manganese Violet

Mars colors (all)
Payne's Gray
Permanent Green, Light and Deep
Prussian Blue
Raw Sienna
Raw Umber
Terra Verte (Green Earth)
Thalo Blue
Thalo Crimson
Thalo Green
Thalo Purple
Thalo Red Rose
Thalo Yellow Green
Thio Violet
Titanium White
Ultramarines (all)
Venetian Red
Viridian
Yellow, Ochre, Light and Deep
Zinc White
Zinc Yellow

Colors that are non-permanent or doubtful are:

Carmine
Chrome Colors (all)
Geranium Lake
Madder Lake
Magenta
Mauve
Scarlet Lake
Turquoise

DRAWING

AN INTRODUCTION TO DRAWING

Drawing has been likened to writing in that it is necessary for the student to master it in order to convey his ideas.

There is no doubt that the student who draws well is free to concentrate on the problem of paint and color, and that poor drawing is a constant stumbling block at every stage of painting. We all hear of artists who, although mediocre draftsmen, are able to hide their lack of that ability with beautiful color, but unfortunately, few of us are gifted with such an eye for color!

I do not believe that the old method of drawing from antique casts for several years, or weeks of drawing a model in the same pose, is an absolute requirement. I think that by constantly sketching and observing the student can master enough of the rudiments of drawing to be able to paint well.

This sketching can be of the things that are around us —homely kitchen utensils, furniture, the view from a window, people at work and at play. Vary your sketching, working sometimes in outline, stressing the contour aspect of drawing. At other times concentrate on light and shade. The main thing is to keep drawing.

If it is not possible to go to an art school, join an art club. Most clubs devote at least one night a week to drawing from a model. Take advantage of such a class. If there are no art clubs available, start an art group among any of your friends who are interested in sketching.

Perspective

For the student of landscape painting some knowledge of perspective is necessary. Concerned with creating a three-dimensional quality on a flat two-dimensional surface, we use perspective as an aid in achieving this effect. The two principal forms of perspective, parallel and angular, help to create the illusion of depth.

In parallel perspective, one vanishing point is used, and all lines parallel to each other converge to this point.

In angular perspective, lines which are at right angles to each other converge to separate points.

The horizon, to which all these lines converge, is always at the level of your eye.

In painting landscapes or seascapes you will soon develop a visual perspective, a "feeling" for the recession of forms. You will still want to check that the objects appearing in your composition converge properly to the eye level. With many artists, as they progress the design of the painting becomes of paramount importance, and to strengthen the impact of design they distort the perspective.

The Basic Forms

A knowledge of the basic forms will help you to see correctly. As you look at an object, no matter how complicated it may seem, the first step is to reduce it to its basic form. Once this "seeing" of the form is established you will be able to draw the object correctly.

The basic forms or models are cubes, cylinders, spheres, hexagons, cones, hemispheres, and pyramids.

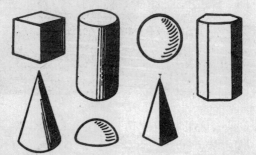

It is only a short step to recognition of the basic forms when sketching from nature. — And then to the head and figure.

FIGURE DRAWING

Even if you are primarily interested in landscape painting, you should be able to depict incidental figures to give
a feeling of life to the subject. The figure is a foil to a
landscape, and if it is not executed convincingly it can
destroy the effect of an otherwise good canvas.

Life drawing should be a part of your training, and, if
possible, should be acquired in an art school. However,
you can learn to draw the figure well by sketching people
at every opportunity. Sketch people in the subway, in the
park, at home, at play. Draw at all times.

Observe how people walk, sit, and stand; notice their
gestures. You will discover that you can often identify
someone you know at a distance by the way his head rests
on his shoulders, and you will see the different postures of
the old and the young. Make notes on how clothes are
draped on a person, and how wrinkles form in a sleeve
when the arm is bent, raised, and hanging at the side.

The drawings do not have to be large—from 2 to 6 inches
will do. They will probably have to be small if you are
trying to capture any action. Indicate the line of action

first and then draw the figure around it. Some of your early attempts may resemble scribbling, but get the action.

Obtain a small sketch pad that can fit into your pocket or purse and carry it with you at all times. Fill the pages with sketches, using a pencil, a fountain pen, or the newer felt-tip pen. If you use a pencil, don't use an eraser. You are not out to collect neat pads of figure drawings. If the line is not right redraw a corrected heavier line over it.

The advantage of using a pen is that it leads to a more direct handling. But do not be concerned about technical handling of the pen. Put the lines down as you feel them. Observe how the shape of a suit or a dress is affected by the figure.

In time your pads will contain a collection of both action sketches and studies of form. As these pads are filled you will develop your figure drawing and acquire enough knowledge to place a single figure or a group of figures convincingly in your composition.

While constant sketching will increase your powers of observation and general facility in handling incidental figures, some time should be spent learning at least the rudiments of anatomy. Study bone and muscle structure, so that you acquire a knowledge of how it affects the figure. It is not essential to know all of the anatomical designations, but you should be able to identify and know the function of the main bones and muscles. You should know the relative proportions of the male and female figure. Most important is to know the working of the movable masses, that is, the head, the rib cage (chest), and the pelvis.

There is no substitute for drawing the figure from life, but you can get a great deal of help from wooden or plastic manikins, which are for sale at most art shops. They can be studied to advantage by checking with an anatomy book in arranging the various positions.

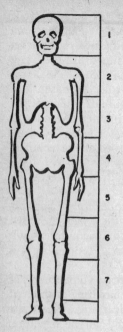

Make simplified drawings of the skeleton so that you acquire a working knowledge of its structure. Pay particular attention to the relative proportions of the head, the rib cage, and the pelvic area, the important masses of the body. Observe how the arms are attached to the shoulder blades and the legs to the sockets of the pelvis.

Notice how the head, the rib cage, and the pelvis are connected by the spine. It is most important to learn how the three masses relate to each other as the figure assumes various positions.

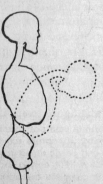

The stick-figure approach to sketching the figure is an old but reliable method. You can achieve far more action in your sketches by using the stick figure as a start in attempting to capture movement. By roughly indicating head, rib cage, and pelvic areas, more resemblance to the human figure can be shown. It is only a short step, then, to reshaping the arms and legs to complete the figure.

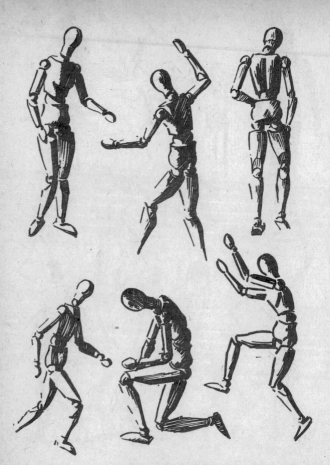

USING A MANIKIN

A manikin can be a big help in figure drawing. There are several types available, and two popular models are shown here. On this page is a manikin that is useful for anatomical study and for experiments with light as an aid in revealing form.

These are sketches of a manikin designed to show the plane structure of the figure. You can learn a great deal about the large
masses of the figure by placing the manikin in various positions.

51

DRAWING
FROM LIFE

The main lines of the figure are sketched in with charcoal.

The modeling of the large forms is broadly indicated as they turn away from the light. Check carefully with the model before rendering. Use the flat side of a small piece of charcoal when drawing the dark areas.

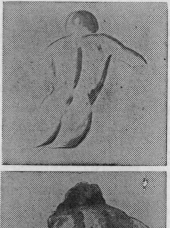

With the large areas of dark and light determined, you now can concentrate on the more subtle forms within these areas. Model them with care, constantly checking to see that they are not overdone, that they keep their place within the large areas.

THE PAINTER'S APPROACH

The figure study below shows the painter's approach. Emphasis is placed on the tonal values as they would appear when painting the figure, rather than those of a line drawing.

Left: The action of the figure is shown by drawing the main lines.

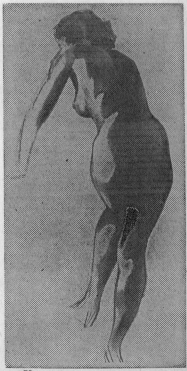

Above: The shaded areas are roughly indicated with the flat side of a piece of charcoal.

Right: The rough areas are rubbed into the paper; the fingers and a rag are used to smooth the charcoal. The study is not one of a detailed search for form but rather one of the distribution of light and shadow.

These two pages are examples of practicing what I preach. Below are some pencil sketches that I made while serving in the Armed Forces. They were done quickly in a small 5-x-8 inch notebook that I kept with me.

The reproductions on the opposite page are sketches I made as a student—quite a few years ago! I sketched people waiting for a bus, shopping, walking; I made notes wherever I saw people gathered.

I believe that this type of figure sketching, opportunities for which are easily available to everyone, is of immeasurable value to all painters.

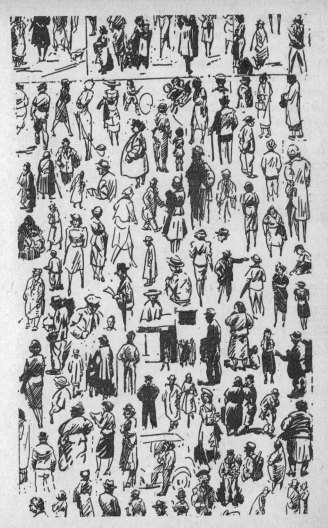

Along with fresh air and sunshine, bathing beaches certainly offer abundant material for studying the human
figure. The sketches on these two pages were made with a
felt-tipped pen on smooth paper. They are not large;
4 inches high is the average size.

Keep in mind an-
atomical   details
when sketching the
figure.

Although drawing must be a depiction of form from a three-dimensional object, the flat surface of a television screen can be used to advantage in studying arrangement. The arrangement can be of a compositional nature or of light-and-shade effects. Figures and animals in motion, which would be almost impossible to sketch directly from life, can be captured by concentrated observation of television.

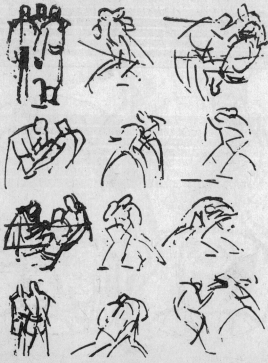

THE THREE BASIC STEPS IN MAKING
A PENCIL DRAWING FROM LIFE

Step 1.

The gesture of the pose is sketched in sweeping lines.

Step 2.

The modeling of the contours starts, following the form of the figure.

Step 3.

The modeling of the contours continues, and at the same time the arrangement of light and dark is rendered.

THE APPROACH TO DRAWING THE SUBJECT

Locate the big masses of your subject first by lightly indicating the main lines. These light lines will act as a guide in sketching in the objects that make up your drawing.

The amount of detail that is to be delineated is determined by what you are striving for. If the drawing is made directly on canvas for a painting to be made on the spot, only the main construction lines are needed. Details can then be added by painting and a freer impression achieved. If a great many details are drawn before painting is begun, a tightness often results.

On the other hand, if you are making a drawing as a means of gathering data for a painting to be done later in the studio, put in as much detail as possible. It can be simplified as you sketch it on the canvas and the drawing can be referred to as you paint. Again, you may do a subject just for the sake of pure drawing. You may wish to express a tonal quality and go to great lengths in studying the minute effects of light and shade. Or you may prefer a more simple rendering, a brief statement of the subject. Experiment constantly. Try various approaches. If you are unsure of your drawing, take time out to correct mistakes as you go along.

Don't be concerned about a clean, neat, finished effect—draw to acquire knowledge, not pictures. On the other hand, if you become too slipshod in your drawing you may need to discipline yourself. Try using a hard, sharply pointed pencil for a while. Your efforts may seem too tight at first, particularly in contrast to what you have been doing, but the final results should eliminate slovenly handling. A hard pencil is also a good remedy for any superficial slickness you may have acquired. Its hard, unyielding line will not permit the dazzling surface performance that is so much more easily accomplished with a soft pencil or a stick of charcoal.

Use your pencil as a guide to proportion by holding it at arm's length, measuring depth and width from the end of the pencil to your thumb. This method is known as "sight measurement." You will also find a pencil an excellent means of checking the angle of receding lines in freehand perspective. It is surprising how many times a receding line appears at first glance to be going downward when actually it is going upward.

Sketch At All Times

STILL-LIFE PAINTING

AN INTRODUCTION TO STILL-LIFE PAINTING

Still-life painting is a complete and fascinating subject in itself, but it is also an excellent exercise for the inexperienced student preparatory to painting outdoors.

Many of the problems that arise when painting landscapes can be solved by still-life practice. Along with improving your knowledge of drawing, you learn the mixing and handling of your paint and brushes. Every type of texture can be studied by a careful selection of the objects to be painted. Silk, with its hard, shining lights, and the heavy, dull, absorbent quality of velvet can be observed as they form the draped background of your subject. Common kitchen objects contain a wealth of shapes and textures to be captured on canvas. Flowers, fruit, and vegetables abound with both obvious and subtle color. Books, lamps, furniture—everything found in your home can be incorporated into pleasing subjects.

You can create your own compositions, lighting effects, and arrangements of color. The important thing is that all these vital ingredients of successful painting can be studied and solved leisurely. Then, when you paint outdoors and the effects are fleeting, you will be better prepared to cope with them, having had some technical experience. Many students find still-life painting dull, probably because they resent the discipline entailed and are unable to sustain their interest. To counteract such boredom, study the masters, both old and modern, and notice how many of their most important works are of still lifes. Look at masterpieces of portraiture in which still-life accessories are employed, and see how important they are to the painting.

STILL-LIFE BACKGROUNDS

In his eagerness to paint the objects in his still-life arrangements, the student very frequently neglects the background. Just as long as the background fits into the color scheme he is content. Actually, the background is just as vital to the success of the painting as the objects being portrayed.

Since drapery affords the most variety and its arrangement as well as its color can be controlled by the painter, some time should be spent in studying it as background material.

Place a few tacks in the upper edge of a piece of material and let it hang freely, assuming its own folds. Notice where the folds are straight and others are V-shaped. Experiment with various types of material, learning how soft heavy cloth hangs in contrast to stiff, shiny material. Try various arrangements of light objects against dark drapery and reverse combinations.

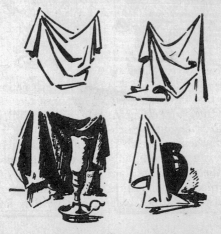

COMPOSITIONAL NOTES PREPARATORY TO PAINTING A STILL LIFE

Various compositions of the still-life subject should always precede the actual painting. They can be made with charcoal applied lightly to the canvas, and can be changed by merely dusting the charcoal lines with a rag or a chamois. The disadvantage of working directly on the canvas, however, is that the composition is lost when changes are made or a fresh one is started. Instead, you can set up your still life in several arrangements and make a rough pencil or charcoal composition of each in your sketchbook. They can be made smaller, but proportional to your canvas. Then select the arrangement you think is the most interesting and redraw it on the canvas.

On the left are shown simple preliminary compositional notes for the still-life demonstration on page 68.

The amount of detail in preliminary compositional notes depends upon the complexity of the still-life arrangement.

STILL-LIFE DEMONSTRATIONS

A Still-Life Study in Oil

In this demonstration of a flower study, the preliminary toning of the values is omitted. Instead, we go directly into color as soon as the composition is indicated with a rough outline of thin French Ultramarine.

After some pencil notes are made of various compositions, the most pleasing is placed on the canvas.

The approximate colors are painted directly on the canvas. Do not attempt to hold your color tightly within the boundaries of the drawn outline. Paint freely, concentrating only on the colors.

The completed study is shown above. Alizarin Crimson, Cadmium Red
Light and a touch of Cobalt Blue are used for the flowers. The leaves
are Thalo Green and Cobalt Blue with touches of Yellow Ochre and Burnt
Sienna. The vase is painted with grays produced with mixtures of Cobalt
Blue, and small amounts of Alizarin Crimson, Yellow Ochre, and Ivory
Black. The table is Cadmium Yellow Light and Yellow Ochre, with accents
of the latter and Burnt Sienna. A mixture of Cobalt Blue, Yellow Ochre,
and Alizarin Crimson is used for the tablecloth and the background, with
the Alizarin Crimson dominating the latter. The white drape shadows are
Cobalt Blue with a touch of Alizarin Crimson.

A Still Life with Water Color

Painting a still life with water color requires a more direct handling of the color than painting one with oil. Preliminary washes of color can be applied, but subsequent washes should be made in a direct, crisp manner. Any fumbling will give the painting a muddy or overworked look. Always mix more color than you think you will use. This will insure more freedom when handling color washes.

A pencil drawing is made with the highlights indicated.

Washes of the approx- imate colors are applied over the objects.

Cadmium Yellow Light is used for the bananas and grapefruit, and for the background curtain. A touch of Cadmium Red Light is added to the yellow for the oranges. This mixture, plus Alizarin Crimson and a touch of Thalo Green, is used for the apples. The grapes are Cobalt Blue with a touch of Alizarin Crimson, and the shadow areas of the tablecloth are a lighter mixture of the same colors. The jug is Yellow Ochre and Burnt Sienna and the background a mixture of the same colors plus Thalo Green.

THE THREE PRINCIPAL STEPS IN PAINTING
A STILL LIFE IN OIL

Step 1. A drawing of the subject is made. It is strengthened by painting the outline with French Ultramarine, Yellow Ochre, or any fairly fast-drying color that is harmonious with the subject.

Step 2. With the same color used for the outline, the arrangement of light and shade is indicated. The paint should be as thin as possible for this.

Step 3. The shaded areas are painted in their approximate colors, then the light areas follow. With the entire canvas covered, the relationship of light and dark areas is checked. The details are then added to complete the painting.

PAINTING AND SKETCHING
OUTDOORS

PAINTING OUTDOORS

Before Starting Out

Check Your Equipment

Make certain that all the colors you will need are in your paint box. There is nothing worse than finally finding an ideal subject after a long trip and discovering that the white paint is missing! Check your brushes, too, and make sure you have enough paint rags.

Always Carry a Reserve Panel

Paint boxes are designed to carry two to three panels. Carry at least one extra panel even though you intend to limit yourself to a single painting. If you get off to a poor start it is better to discard the canvas for the moment, since reworking into a wet canvas generally produces muddy color. And a fresh panel with its inviting white surface will be more of an inspiration to start fresh. The light may change drastically when you are halfway through a painting. Rather than attempt to adjust the painting to a cloudy sky or some other change, start a new canvas.

Travel As Lightly As Possible

If you have a considerable amount of walking to do to reach your sketching spot, travel as lightly as possible. To be exhausted by the time you are ready to paint certainly will not help you to produce your best work. The easel can often be temporarily dispensed with if you are working on a panel size that will fit your paint box. If the weather permits, a newspaper can be substituted for a sketching stool, or you might even find a convenient rock to sit on.

Dress Appropriately for the Outdoors

It is not at all necessary to go to extremes—avoiding white clothes, for instance, because light cloth can reflect into a painting and affect the color—but you should dress sensibly for the season of the year. It does not take long to lose enthusiasm when you are shivering while painting a winter subject on a cold day. And you will be less subject to eyestrain as well as heat if you wear a hat with a brim or a peak during the summer.

Starting Out

The primary advantage of painting or sketching outdoors is that nature is constantly supplying fresh ideas, color schemes, hitherto unseen details, and the passing effect of many moods. The painter's imagination is constantly stimulated. Select a time of day when the light is interesting and fairly steady. Whether you complete your painting in one sitting or return to the spot on successive days depends upon both your technical ability and what you are attempting to do. A fleeting effect has to be captured at one time, but an exhaustive study, or series of studies, can be made for several days. Of course, the weather and the season of the year are vital factors.

Always carry a small pad with you on which to make preliminary pencil or pen compositions. Make several sketches —they can be rough and do not have to be large—2 x 3 inches will suffice. This is time well spent, for a pleasing composition will excite and sustain interest in the subject until it is completed on the canvas.

Some examples of preliminary compositions are shown on the following page.

THE THREE BASIC RULES
FOR WORKING OUTDOORS

1. Determine your horizon line, making sure that all your receding lines converge properly. Sketch the general contours of the big shapes. Keep them fairly angular and avoid drawing details too soon.

2. The same advice applies to shading. Indicate the large masses first, in simple light and shade. Avoid using half-tones at this stage. Watch your source of light and keep it consistent.

3. Put in the half-tones, constantly checking the relationship of the light and dark values. Then render the details and necessary accents in the final stage to complete the picture.

The black and white sketches
shown above are pages from my
notebook of New England.

SIMPLIFY!

Do not attempt to depict every detail

but SUGGEST

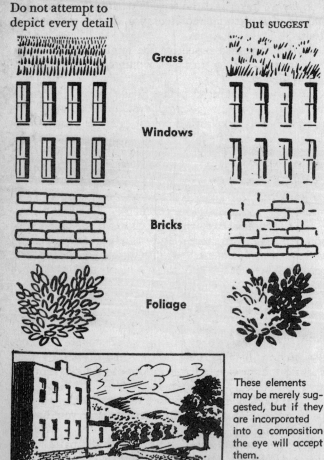

Grass

Windows

Bricks

Foliage

These elements may be merely suggested, but if they are incorporated into a composition the eye will accept them.

THE SKETCH VERSUS THE STUDY

So far we have used the term "sketching" to mean the making of a pictorial representation that is complete in itself.

We have avoided rendering the minute details, being interested only in capturing a spontaneous interpretation of the subject.

Along with making sketches, time should be taken to make studies. Since we plan eventually to work our sketches into larger finished paintings in the studio, some details of the various objects that make up the composition may be needed. For example, if you have a large tree in the immediate foreground you will need more than just an impression of the tree. The bark may possess an interesting textural quality. Take the time to make a detailed study of the bark formation.

If large rocks occupy an important part of your sketch, you will have to do more than just indicate them in light and shade. Supplementary studies should be made so that rough and smooth areas, crevices, moss stain, and other details are recorded.

Studies should be made of subtle color effects. Occasionally just paint the color passage of the foreground area. At other times concentrate on the sky alone. You will find that there are times when the scene before you does not produce much inspiration. Instead of wasting time waiting or hoping for a more receptive mood, single out an area and make a study of it.

Tight black-and-white studies, rendered with pencil or pen, are excellent disciplinary exercises if you have a tendency to work carelessly.

Whether you make studies for later studio paintings or just as a discipline, you will find them well worth the time spent.

THE VIEW-FINDER

A view-finder is a mechanical aid for the painter. It is simply a piece of cardboard with a rectangular opening in it that corresponds roughly to the proportions of your canvas. Assuming that you are working on a 12-x-16-inch panel, the opening would be 3 x 4 inches. A margin of a few inches around the opening will suffice for blocking-out purposes. By focusing the finder on the subject before you, moving it up and down or from left to right, you can select what you think is the most pleasing arrangement. The margin of the finder blocks off enough of the scene to allow you to concentrate on what you see through the opening. You will have use for the finder only during the planning of the composition. Once this has been arrived at the finder can be put back in your paint box, thumb-tacked to the inside of the lid for safe-keeping. Some painters paint their view-finders black to give them a definitely concentrated contrast in their selection of the arrangement.

You will have to squint or close one eye when focusing and vary the distance when holding the finder, depending on the amount of subject matter you wish to include.

The scene in its entirety, before using the view-finder.

Cropping the mountains
makes the foreground im-
portant.

A vertical arrangement emphasizes
the figure.

Interest is concentrated
on the middle and fore-
ground by cropping the
sky.

Centering the view-finder
gives all the elements
equal importance.

ATMOSPHERIC EFFECT

When sketching outdoors we soon become conscious of a blue tone or haze that seems to envelop the distant objects in the landscape. This is particularly noticeable when there are hills or mountains in the distance. The more distant they are the bluer they become.

We soon discover that colors are affected by aerial, sometimes referred to as atmospheric, perspective. Colors become grayer and bluer as they recede. Of the basic primary colors it is yellow that first diminishes in intensity. This becomes evident when we observe hills. Assume that we are doing a summer subject and all the hills are covered with green foliage. There is no mistaking the green of the hill close to us, for the yellow is still apparent, but as the hills recede the yellow gradually disappears and the blue predominates. The next color to diminish is red. An example is immediately apparent in a mountain subject. As the violet mountains go farther back, the red evaporates and the distant range becomes blue. In turn, the blue is affected by the atmospheric quality and becomes lighter, finally vanishing in the haze.

The picture opposite is a simplified illustration of aerial values. It is important to remember that sharp edges come forward and soft edges recede, and to add your details in the shadow areas, not in the light.

Although the illustration has been reduced to just black, and three grays, more intermediate tones of gray could be added.

You may wish to use some of your discarded landscape sketches to experiment with the recession of color as it is affected by the atmosphere. Select a sketch—it can be oil, water color, or pastel—whose chief fault lies in its being off in tonal values. Outline in warm colors the objects and large forms that are close to you. In the middle distance start using cooler colors, until the far distance is rendered with just a faint blue outline which finally disappears completely.

The outline does not have to envelop each shape entirely. Rather, use a "lost-and-found" line. When completing the altered sketch you will immediately perceive how the warm outline shapes come forward and the cool ones recede.

GETTING THE MOST OUT OF A SUBJECT

If you find a subject that stimulates you, get the most out of it. Study it in various lights—in the morning light, for instance, as compared with the warmer late afternoon. Although noon gives the most unflattering light, the subject may be one that lends itself to the best interpretation at that time. I have favorite subjects that I return to time and again. Along with studying them under varying lighting conditions, I return at different seasons of the year to paint them and discover new inspiration.

SOLVING EACH PROBLEM AS IT ARISES

If you find that drawing a particular subject is difficult for you, do not rush into painting with the desperate hope that the application of color will solve everything. Instead, make your small preliminary compositions, select one, and spend the rest of the time drawing it on the canvas. You can outline it with French Ultramarine, checking the drawing constantly, and conclude by giving some thought to the light and shadow areas.

Keep thinking about the subject—its arrangement, its color, how you are going to interpret it—and the next day return to the same spot. You have already solved the problem of drawing it to the best of your ability. Now you have the full sitting in which to concentrate on the painting. You will make better progress by isolating each problem, finding the best possible solution to it, and then tackling the next one.

This is a procedure that insures progress, and it is one that many professional artists follow. They will work a long time on a single theme—anything from a still life containing a textural problem to nocturnes. It can be subject matter of a religious nature, a scene in a foreign country, or the lighting effect on a particular surface. Whatever the subject, the professional artist makes exhaustive studies of it. When he feels that he has interpreted the subject to the extent of his capabilities he may have a one-man exhibition whose theme is the solution of the problem. It is surprising how few people who view the paintings realize this; most regard it simply as subject matter that has appealed to the artist. This can be partly true, but only the artist knows to what extent he has met the challenge of solving his particular problem.

PAINTING LIGHT AND SHADOW

• The placing of a cast shadow will often give interest and mystery to what would otherwise be a monotonous area.

• By using a more vivid color as an accent along the edges of the light area where they meet the shadows, the sunny effect is heightened.

• Another way to avoid having cast shadows appear too heavy is to place strong dark accents within the shadow areas. The contrast makes the cast shadow seem lighter and a feeling of luminosity is imparted.

• An objectionable foreground can often be minimized by introducing a cast shadow in the immediate foreground. This shadow is also a good device for focusing the spectator's interest into the middle-ground area when desired.

• In painting a sunny subject, the glaring light striking some of the objects appears to be pure white. Put a touch of Light Yellow or Yellow Ochre in the white paint and it will accentuate the feeling of glare.

• Watch the cast shadows on areas such as roads and flat rooftops. Keep in mind that the light falling from the sky penetrates these shadows, adding to their luminosity.

• Shadows often appear to be very dark, particularly on a bright, glaring day, and students frequently paint them too heavily. Keep in mind that the shadows always contain a certain amount of reflected light and paint them accordingly.

• Just painting the shadow areas alone gives the viewer a comprehensive realization of the subject. In continuing the painting, place the details and accents in these shadow areas and keep the light area fairly flat and simple. A surprisingly strong interpretation of the subject will result.

• The shapes and colors of shadows are most interesting to paint in late-afternoon or early-morning light.

• Indicate all the shadow areas at the same time, so that they are truly related to one another. If you paint them piecemeal, by the time the entire canvas is covered the angle of light will have changed their length.

Because trees form one of the most important elements in landscape painting, much time should be spent studying them. While it is not necessary to be able to identify every tree by name, the painter should become thoroughly familiar with their characteristics. Their anatomy can be more thoroughly studied in the late autumn or winter when they are bare of leaves.

A typical example is the difference in the trunks of trees. Generally a fast-growing tree is much straighter than a slow-growing one. Notice how the branches leave the trunk, so that you will have some knowledge of what is taking place when you paint the tree in full leaf at a later date. The notes you make when the trees are bare will aid in understanding how the masses or clusters of green leaves

Summer

are formed by the under-structure.

When drawing or painting the foliage of the tree, look for the large masses first. Try to see the entire tree as broadly as possible. After indicating the largest masses, look for the secondary forms within these masses. Disregard the leaves—squint your eyes so that you see only the general masses.

Keep the mass effect in mind at all times when you are painting in color. Choose a time of day when the light and shade areas are clearly visible, to help you to define the big shapes.

Avoid the obvious green used by inexperienced painters. Study the clusters of trees before you, noticing how some are more bluish than others. Observe that what at first seemed to be a definite green in a neighboring tree really has a yellowish cast, while another may run to more brown.

The Same Subject in Autumn

Exaggerate these colors when you apply them to the canvas, and it is surprising how readily your eye will accept them as an interesting group of trees. Your first efforts may contain some raw color but you will soon learn to modify it. By using this approach in painting trees you will avoid the deadly monotony of obvious green.

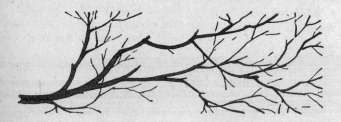

• Study a branch in your studio. Take special note of the angles—of how the smaller branches leave the larger one. Note the gradual tapering toward the ends of the twigs.

• Add a decorative note to the subject by composing a painting so that the trees form a frame.

• The spots of sky that are seen breaking through a tree are often painted too light. When we look at these spots and see them enveloped by dark green leaves the contrast often exaggerates the light that penetrates. In order to keep these spots from "jumping out" of the tree, paint them in a slightly lower key than the rest of the sky. The smaller the spot, the lower the key.

• When painting a group of trees, look for a light tree against a darker tree to add variety to the scene.

• You will find it helpful to draw a tree as it grows, from the base upward, from trunk to branch to twig. The area that it is to occupy can be lightly indicated, but when doing the actual drawing start at the base working upward and outward to the tips.

• Try to convey the feeling that the base of your tree is really growing out of the ground, with its roots gripping the earth. Many beginners paint their trees as if they were upright logs, cut sharply and flush with the ground.

• Avoid painting a clear, definite line where the tree meets the grass; soften the edge instead. Notice how the grass is reflected upon the tree trunk and paint some of this green into the trunk.

• An excellent exercise is to make as many compositions as possible using the same tree as a motif. You will learn how a tree can be a complete composition in itself, how the tree can influence the foreground, how it can become a subordinate element in a vista, how it can guide the eye to the middle ground or the distance.

• Mistakes are frequently made in drawing the branches emerging from the main limbs. Remember that the branches grow in different directions from the limbs.

• Simplify the modeling of the trees as they recede by limiting the tonal range.

• Watch the edges of your foliage; a sharply defined edge comes forward and a soft edge recedes.

The Silhouette Reveals the Identity
of the Tree

While the silhouette reveals the identity of the tree, keep in mind
the importance of its depth. Take pains to depict the clustered areas
of leaves that come toward you as well as those that recede.

WATER

Generally the dark areas of an object reflected in water appear slightly grayed and the light areas a bit darker, because water has a neutralizing effect on all reflected color. The amount of neutralization varies according to the intensity of the source of light; it will be more for a dull

Typical reflection on a calm day.

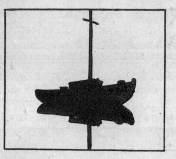

Same reflection affected by wind.

gray sky than for a bright blue one.

On an absolutely still day the reflection will be mirror-like. Any breeze that blows, however slight, will cause wavelets that break and distort the shape of the reflection.

If this slight breeze turns into a strong wind the surface of the water is so broken that the ripples become surging waves, completely destroying the reflection.

• Notice the sky when you are painting a lake, a river, or any inland water. The color of the sky will generally determine the color of the water.

• When painting the reflections of trees, paint the foliage first and then the branches.

• Notice the line of light that is generally seen at the base of the immediate reflections of river banks, shorelines, and even the edges of puddles.

• A body of water varies in color from the immediate foreground to the distant horizon. Its color is affected by the amount and quality of light it receives from its depth, its shallow areas, the sky, prevailing winds, and reflections of its surroundings.

• By using more medium than usual when painting with oil, a more fluid stroke is attended. This is helpful in giving a more liquid look to the water.

• Keep in mind the rules of perspective when rendering ripples or wavelets, which should become deeper as they come nearer to you.

• When painting water breaking or swirling over rocks, notice how the greenish cast of the water and the foam accents the reddish tinge of the projecting rocks.

• When painting a rocky coastline, make frequent use of the palette knife for depicting the rocks. The knife helps to achieve the rugged textural quality of the rock. Keep the undertones warm, working up to the local color.

The sky creates the mood of the landscape. It determines the quality of light that permeates the entire subject. Normally lighter at the horizon, the sky gradually becomes deeper overhead.

However, it is not until cloud formations appear that a feeling of movement is imparted to a painting, and the painting of clouds is a major problem for many students. They load the canvas with white paint, hoping to capture the fleeting effect before them, and the clouds soon take on a chalky, overworked look with no semblance of atmospheric quality. Clouds are not as white as they first appear to be. They must be carefully observed and the lost-and-found quality of their edges determined, then they can be composed into the sky area to strengthen the entire design of the painting.

It would be wise to make, first, several pencil drawings of the various formations so that some knowledge is acquired of their anatomy. At the same time study their values. Notice that the smaller, wispy clouds are darker in value as compared to the larger, heavier clouds. Follow this period of drawing by painting cloud studies, again observing that the smaller clouds are cooler in color when contrasted to the warmer tone of the larger clouds.

Some painters apply a toning of yellow ochre and white over the entire sky area. They then paint the sky, leaving the toning the shape of the cloud formations. The clouds are then lightened and modeled to the degree desired. This method helps avoid the chalkiness that is so often found in students' work.

As you continue to work and observe you will discover that, while the clouds are constantly changing, a certain pattern does exist. The formation will never be exactly the same, but the pattern will help you to establish a convincing rendering of the clouds.

• There is no definite rule as to when the sky should be painted in the development of the subject, but since the sky is the key to the landscape, it should constantly be compared to the rest of the subject to determine the degree of contrast in color values. A water-colorist may prefer to do the sky first, because it is easier to paint any intricate dark shapes over the sky area than to paint the sky around the shapes. On the other hand, a painter using oil may just indicate a few strokes of the sky value overhead, a few more at the horizon, and then concentrate on covering the landscape area. He can work on the sky again later and design cloud forms to fit the over-all composition. Whatever approach you use, always keep checking the relationship of the sky to the landscape.

• When clouds are painted high in the sky the objects below appear shorter. When painted lower, toward the horizon, the clouds impart a feeling of majestic height to the objects.
• The rawness of the blue that is found in so many students' skies can be modified with Raw Umber or Light

Red. A touch of either color added to the blue mixture will neutralize the color.

• A more "atmospheric" quality can be given to blue skies in a water color by first laying a light Umber wash over the sky area. Allow it to dry before applying the blue.

• When the landscape is flat and uninteresting, have the sky dominate the composition. Stress the cloud formation, making it as exciting and interesting as possible.

• Clouds offer a ready means to express recession in your painting. They are the most flexible element in the composition.

• Use cloud forms as an aid in designing the picture.

Opposite is shown one of several methods of painting clouds and sky. The clouds are quickly sketched in when an interesting formation takes place, the modeling of their forms follows, and the color of the sky is painted last.

PROCEDURE IN PAINTING CLOUDS AND SKY

Step 1.

The drawing.

Step 2.

The lay-in of the cloud forms.

Step 3.

The painting of the sky.

FOREGROUND

• Take care not to make the general tone of the foreground too dark, especially if it is in shadow. It should always be luminous enough so that dark objects can be discerned and sharp accents defined.

• Broken color and paint applied in an impasto manner will impart a textural quality.

• Because aerial perspective controls the degree of local color, objects closer to you will be stronger in color.

• The view-finder described on page 80 will be a great help in determining the amount of foreground to include in the painting.

• If your foreground has a tendency to become fuzzy or overworked, some touches of paint applied with the palette knife will give it an immediate feeling of crisp vitality.

• Avoid placing a figure in full light in the immediate foreground unless you want the landscape reduced to secondary interest.

• Be careful not to distort objects. A bush that is close to you will resemble a tree if allowance is not made for the distorted perspective.

• By establishing the base line of your subject a bit higher, an objectionable immediate foreground can often be eliminated.

• It is necessary to render a certain amount of detail to bring the foreground toward you, but do not overdo it. Too much detail will prevent the viewer's eye from traveling over the entire composition.

OIL-PAINTING DEMONSTRATIONS

The demonstrations that follow are necessarily broken down into stages to show the gradual painting of the subject. After you have been painting for some time, you will realize the danger of painting by a formula, and what I am trying to show in these demonstrations is just one approach out of many that could be applied to the particular subject. It is meant to give a method of keeping the subject under control throughout the painting, to help the beginner avoid what I have seen happen to many amateurs, who work hard at painting for a while, only to give up in disgust. Some load the canvas so heavily with unwieldy paint in trying to capture the color before them that they get a muddy effect. Others apply the paint so thinly that the result is a sad, weak, washed-out presentation. Still others are in such a hurry to start painting that they neglect the preliminary drawing or composition and the subject becomes unrecognizable.

These demonstrations illustrate a planned procedure for constructive painting. A drawing is made or some definition of the lines of the composition is indicated. This is followed by a toned indication of light and shade, and then by the application of color. This approach may vary with some subjects under the conditions shown.

By separating the subject into these various stages you tackle one problem at a time, giving yourself a chance to isolate and solve each problem in a way that allows the gradual development of the painting.

The following demonstrations show some methods that can be used in developing a painting. They have been painted expressly for this book to give you an idea of the construction that precedes the surface effect of the finished painting. Although the technical aspect of the finished work cannot be neglected, the beginner should be more concerned with the construction than with acquiring a technique as soon as possible. As you work and experiment you will gradually develop a technique that will permit you to express yourself. In this use "technique" may be compared to handwriting—it is the surface brushwork interpretation of the subject. However, the technical aspect of the proper mixing of colors, the use of painting media and surfaces, the knowledge of permanent and fugitive colors, and so on should be learned as early as possible. In other words, be a good workman by learning your craft well from the start.

There are two ways of approaching oil painting, as shown in these demonstrations. In one method the entire painting is usually executed in one session, without any of the passages being allowed to dry. The surface is always wet, because the colors are applied directly to the canvas or over one another. This is known as "alla prima."

The other method is to paint areas or passages and allow them to dry thoroughly before repainting over the same area. The preliminary painting should always be done thinly and the subsequent painting gradually applied more heavily, to help avoid future cracking of the paint layers. This procedure has many advantages over the first method, because it makes it easier to maintain control of the painting. The painting surfaces can gradually be built up and many interesting textures developed. In the process of drying some of the color passages may turn dull and need to be sprayed with a bit of retouch varnish before the area is repainted. This will restore the color and provide a better surface for subsequent painting. The disadvantage of the second method is the chance of the painting becoming "cold"—that is, losing both your interest and the spirit of the subject. In contrast, the alla prima method insures spontaneity and a more fluent effect.

Try both ways of painting. Your temperament or the subject may determine how you want to work. In any event, most of the times that you paint on the spot directly from nature you will want to complete the painting in one session. If you decide later on to make a large studio painting from the spot sketch, you can then work more deliberately, planning each step and taking as much time as necessary to complete the painting.

Most of the subjects chosen for the following demonstrations were painted under strong sunlight; consequently the student can grasp the arrangement of light and shadow with little difficulty. The subjects are also of tangible substance rather than pure landscapes, thus simplifying the problem of drawing and subsequent painting. To get the most out of these demonstrations, pick similar subjects, and use the approach suggested in paintings of your own. As you progress, you will gradually develop your own approaches to particular subjects.

Sketch At All Times

THE THREE PRINCIPAL STEPS
IN PAINTING A LANDSCAPE IN OIL

The three principal steps in producing an oil painting are the drawing of the subject, the arrangement of light and shade, and the application of color. The amount of detail necessary in the drawing depends upon the subject. Either charcoal or pencil can be used.

As you progress you will undoubtedly eliminate many of the smaller details and merely indicate the large masses. The amount of drawing needed for the average subject is shown below. The arrangement of light and shade follows. This is generally indicated by using French Ultramarine, which is applied very thinly so that it does not noticeably affect the subsequent coloring.

Shown opposite is the painting completed in color. Do not be concerned if the blue paint used in the previous step shows through. That is why we use blue—it helps the atmospheric quality of landscape painting.

The drawing.

The arrangement of light and shade.

Colors used for principal objects (white paint is added wherever needed).

Sky: Thalo Blue with a touch of French Ultramarine.

Sidewalk and Street: Yellow Ochre, Ivory Black, French Ultramarine, Alizarin Crimson.

Telegraph Poles: Burnt Sienna, Raw Umber, Alizarin Crimson.

Red Buildings: Alizarin Crimson, Cadmium Red Light.

Buff Buildings: Yellow Ochre, Burnt Sienna.

Green Buildings: Thalo Green, Cadmium Yellow Light.

Store Windows: Alizarin Crimson, French Ultramarine, Ivory Black.

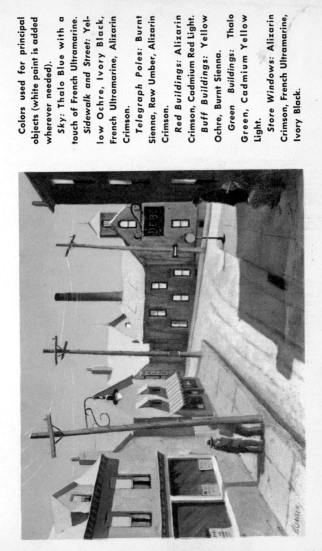

105

Rolling Hills

In this demonstration, the drawing which is the first step is less detailed than in the previous demonstration. As our subject is one of rolling country, with few man-made objects to be depicted, only the big masses are indicated. The lines are kept angular. The subject is then redrawn more accurately with French Ultramarine, using a small brush.

Since we are assuming in this demonstration that we want to capture the effect before us as quickly as possible, we will dispense with the usual blue lay-in and dark arrangement. Instead, we shall go directly into color.

The composition is lightly indicated with charcoal.

The subject is redrawn more accurately with French Ultramarine.

The subject is painted directly in the approximate colors in a loose manner.

Sky: Cobalt Blue, Viridian.

Mountains: Cobalt Blue, Alizarin Crimson.

Fields: Cadmium Yellow Light, Viridian.

Earth: Yellow Ochre, Light Red.

Distant Trees: Cadmium Yellow Deep, Viridian.

Large Tree: Viridian, Cadmium Yellow Deep, Burnt Sienna, Raw Umber.

Fences: Raw Umber, Light Red.

Foreground: Light Red, Viridian, Burnt Sienna, Cadmium Yellow Light.

At the start of this stage the entire canvas has been roughly covered, except for the cloud area and the front of the white house. The original French Ultramarine outline is still visible. Painting proceeds with a more accurate shaping of the various forms. More color is added wherever necessary and the blue outline gradually disappears.

From now to the finish the color is gradually refined along with the brush work. The distant and middleground areas are simplified. Some vivid color is added to the foreground and sunny highlights are rendered on the fence and foliage. Details are added to the walking figure as the painting is completed.

Mountain Country

So far we have shown the use of a comprehensive draw-ing and one with less detail, simply indicated with angular lines preparatory to painting. Now we have a subject in which it is important to capture the quality of rhythm. While it is still simply indicated, we now concentrate on depicting the rhythmic forms in our preliminary drawing. We continue with the French Ultramarine lay-in and make it more realistic but still hold the rhythm of line.

The rhythm of line is stressed in the prelimi-nary drawing on the canvas.

The subject is then more realistically ren-dered, using only French Ultramarine very thinly.

Starting with the foreground, the approximate colors are vigorously brushed in, using Yellow Ochre and Burnt Sienna. The same colors are used, with the addition of Thalo Green, for the middle distance. Still using the same colors, with the addition of Ivory Black to neutralize them, the first mountain range is painted. The French Ultramarine undertone will pick up slightly, contributing a harmonious note to all the colors.

At the start of this stage the unpainted areas of the water in the foreground, as well as the distant mountains and the sky, are still in the original French Ultramarine lay-in. Yellow Ochre, Thalo Green, and French Ultramarine are used for the mountain areas. Water and sky are painted next, using Thalo Green and French Ultramarine to complete this stage.

In this final stage the details are rendered, with warm colors used for accents. Apply the paint thickly in depicting the textural quality of the trees and the bush, and to produce the glaring effect of light on the water.

113

Rocks and Surf

In this subject movement must be captured, and it is important that the surf be indicated in a pleasing arrangement before the painting is begun. Study the subject well before you start your drawing. As you observe the rolling surf you will detect a certain pattern that takes form just before the water breaks over the rocks. Make some preliminary pencil notes to help you establish the surf pattern. Then make the drawing directly with the brush, on the canvas, using French Ultramarine. When you start to paint let the white of the canvas be the surf pattern. The actual painting of the surf does not take place until the final stage. If you attempt to paint it too soon you are likely to become so involved with the constant motion that you will accumulate merely a mass of unwieldy paint.

The drawing is made directly on the canvas with French Ultramarine.

114

Light Red, cut to a thin consistency, is quickly rubbed over the rock area. This is followed by the green hill, a mixture of Viridian and Cadmium Yellow Light. Yellow Ochre is used to indicate the shadows of the sand. The sky is then painted with Viridian and French Ultramarine, with the latter intensified toward the top.

The illustration above shows the water sketchily painted with Viridian and French Ultramarine; the rooftops with Alizarin Crimson and Cadmium Red Light; and lighthouse shadow areas with French Ultramarine, Alizarin Crimson and a touch of Ivory Black. The sand area follows, with Yellow Ochre and Cadmium Yellow Light. Below is the start of the modeling of the rocks, with the shadow area painted with Light Red, French Ultramarine, and a touch of Cadmium Red Light.

The painting of the rocks continues, with occasional use of the palette knife (see page 129) in applying the paint. The knife imparts a feeling of rugged strength to this area. The breaking waves are also rendered with the knife. The painting is concluded with the sharp details depicted with a rigger brush.

117

Harbor Vista

An accurate drawing is necessary in painting a vista because, besides requiring a more ambitious composition, the perspective requires a detailed rendering. Make several small preliminary pencil sketches in your notebook until a suitable composition is obtained. Then make a careful drawing on the canvas. Because the color arrangement is most vital in this subject, we start working directly with paint, indicating the color in the shaded area first. It is surprising how the subject immediately takes on a comprehensive impression with just these areas covered with paint and the light areas remaining the white of the original canvas.

A careful drawing is made of the subject.

The shaded areas are painted first in their approximate colors. The green areas are mixtures of Cadmium Yellow, Light and Deep, with Thalo Green, Light Red and Yellow Ochre added. The shadowed sides of the white houses are painted with Cobalt Blue, Light Red, and occasional touches of Yellow Ochre. The rooftops are Cobalt Blue and Alizarin Crimson. The red areas are mixtures of Light Red and Alizarin Crimson. Yellow Ochre, Thalo Green and Cobalt Blue are used in the distant areas.

With the shaded areas rendered roughly, the middle tone and lighter areas are now painted, still in a loose manner. This loose manner should allow bits of the white canvas to show through until the final stage is reached. The light areas are painted with mixtures of Yellow Ochre, Cadmium Yellow Light, and Light Red.

The entire canvas is gradually covered as the light areas are completed. From now to the finish the usual details are rendered along with the refining and smoothing of the color and brush work. Your sable brushes will be helpful in accomplishing this. The rigger brush will be handy for the needed accents.

Bay Road

As you work you may arrive at a stage in which you are satisfied with the drawing and tonal quality of your paintings but feel that they lack color. Or you may be timid with the use of color, fearing that it will become blatant if you use it boldly. This demonstration shows the use of a bright preliminary or underpainting to insure a vivid finished painting. After the usual drawing is made, the canvas is covered in all except the sunniest areas with a warm interpretation of the local colors. Use enough medium, particularly turpentine, to insure a thin, almost watercolor-like staining of the canvas. The over-all effect will be one of over-bright, verging on gaudy, color. Then paint into this underpainting, while it is still wet, the color you feel it should be. You will discover that the bright underpainting will affect the subsequent color enough to make

it more vivid and rich. You will also find that when you are working directly, with color painted over a wet underpainting, it is easier to tone down a color over a brilliant base than it is to brighten color over a dull color.

The Old Barn

In this section, painting with a palette or painting knife is demonstrated. The use of the knife is described on page 129.

The previous demonstration of Bay Road illustrated one way of obtaining brighter color. Painting with a knife also insures clear, vibrant color; it is the constant brushing of mixed color that so often produces a dull effect. By eliminating the brush and using only a knife a feeling of vitality is immediately imparted to the color on the canvas. It does not matter how much you stir the paint with a knife, it will still remain fresh and clean. Just a brief indication of the composition is needed, as the object of this demonstration is to do all the work with the knife. A direct, broad effect of the subject is our aim. Painting with a knife is also an excellent way to eliminate the tendency to put in unnecessary details.

A simple drawing is made of the subject and roughly outlined with a brush, using French Ultramarine.

Painting with the knife starts with the spotting of various colors. No attempt is made to cover the entire area of each color at this stage. The red barn is a mixture of Cadmium Red Light and Cadmium Yellow Deep, with the roof of the large barn a very light mixture of the same. The foliage is a combination of Cadmium Yellow Light, Thalo Green, and French Ultramarine. Burnt Sienna is used for the warm interiors. The touch of sky is Thalo Blue and the barn and the fence are Cobalt Blue and Light Red.

125

The painting continues, using the same colors and extending the covering of the same areas. The foreground is a mixture of Yellow Ochre, Cadmium Red Light, and Thalo Green. If any difficulty is encountered with unsatisfactory color, do not hesitate to scrape it off and repaint it with the knife.

Gradually cover the canvas, still using the designated colors. Use the knife for painting as long as you can. Since the knife naturally does not have the flexibility of a brush, do not be overconcerned about technique. Just apply the paint, color for color, as you see it. Resort to the rigger brush only for the final sharp accents and details.

Palette-Knife Painting

1. Strokes made with the tip of the knife (foliage, etc.)

2. Strokes applied with a downward motion in graduating tones.

3. Graduating tones applied horizontally are easier to blend for sky, etc.

4. Paint applied in a solid manner and then scraped while still wet.

5. Light paint over wet background for turbulent feeling, water, etc.

6. Scraping after dark paint has become tacky.

7. Paint dabbed on thinly with tip of knife.

8. Shapes scraped into wet background.

9. Light paint applied heavily and allowed to dry. Dark paint then applied flatly, followed by scraping.

PALETTE-KNIFE PAINTING

Painting with the palette knife is an excellent method to acquire a broad handling of oil paint. Any tendency toward tightness or muddy color is overcome when the brushes are put aside for a while and the entire painting is rendered with a knife. Clean, sparkling effects can be achieved, for it is virtually impossible to have the color go muddy or dull as so frequently happens when colors are mixed with a brush.

Your first attempts may be awkward until you have acquired the knack of applying the color to the canvas with the knife. Make certain that the blade is flexible.

The average palette knife is primarily designed for removing the paint from the palette and scraping unwanted color off the canvas. It necessarily has a stiffer blade than that used for painting. What you want is really a "painting knife," which can be obtained in a variety of sizes and shapes.

As you use the knife your work immediately assumes a feeling of vitality. In contrast to brushes, which quickly become stained with color, the knife is easily cleaned with a wipe of the paint rag.

You may find it feasible to combine the knife and the brush for some subjects. Interesting textures can be obtained with this combination; for example, the sky can be painted with the brush and the clouds given more vitality with touches of the knife, or water might be painted smoothly with a brush and the rocks with the knife to give an interesting contrast.

The demonstration on pages 124-127 shows the use of the knife only in the rendering of the subject.

The Lone House

For our initial demonstration of water-color painting a simple subject has been chosen. We will also work with a limited selection of paints, so that you can discover the variety of colors that can be obtained by mixing. The entire picture demonstrated here was painted with eight colors.

First a careful pencil drawing was made of the subject on a sheet of cold-pressed water-color board. Board was chosen for this first demonstration to insure that the surface would not buckle when wet color was applied. This leaves us free to concentrate on the mixing of the necessary colors and the actual painting.

As you progress you will want to experiment with paper instead of board. You will find that paper, although it will occasionally buckle, particularly in the lighter weights, will impart more luminosity and a more pleasing textural quality to your work.

A careful pencil drawing is made of the subject.

A wash of Cadmium Yellow Light is laid over the entire area, except for the sky, and allowed to dry.

Roof, door, shutters, and barrel are painted with a mixture of Cadmium Red Light and Cadmium Yellow Light. This is followed by a wash of Alizarin Crimson over the chimney and Cobalt Blue for the windows. A mixture of Cadmium Yellow Light and Viridian produce the green for the foreground.

131

The sky is painted with French Ultramarine with a touch of Viridian. The shadow side follows, using French Ultramarine and Alizarin Crimson. The latter color is then used for the shaded side of the chimney. The hill area is now given a wash of clear water. While that is still wet, Viridian is floated into it, modeling the form. The same procedure is used for the road and earth areas, with Yellow Ochre used for the modeling. The painting is completed with accents of French Ultramarine in the windows and Burnt Sienna for the shingles, barrel, door and shutters.

132

The Red Barn

The sky is painted immediately after the pencil drawing is made. This is done by wetting the sky area of the paper with clean water and floating the sky and cloud colors into the wet surface, allowing them to blend and impart an atmospheric quality. The subject takes shape as the darks are gradually painted.

Sky: Yellow Ochre and Cobalt Blue.

Barn: Cadmium Red Light, Alizarin Crimson.

Mountain: Cobalt Blue, Alizarin Crimson.

Road and Fields: Yellow Ochre.

House: Davy's Gray; Roof, Cadmium Red Light.

Trees: Cadmium Yellow Light, Thalo Green, Yellow Ochre.

Fence and Dark Areas: Burnt Sienna, Ivory Black, Alizarin Crimson.

134

Maine Boatman

In this subject the two lightest elements, the sky and the water, are painted first. The dark trees and the foreground follow, and a range from light to dark is immediately established. The rest of the picture is then painted, with the sky and the foreground as guides for values.

Clouds: Yellow Ochre and Davy's Gray.

Sky: Cobalt Blue and a touch of Thalo Green.

Water: Same colors, but lighter mixture.

Foreground: Yellow Ochre, Alizarin Crimson, Cobalt Blue.

Trees: Cadmium Yellow Light, Thalo Green, Burnt Sienna, Yellow Ochre.

Shore: Yellow Ochre, Cadmium Yellow Light, Thalo Green.

House: Davy's Gray, Cobalt Blue; roof, Pale Alizarin Crimson.

Mountains: Cobalt Blue, Alizarin Crimson.

Boat: Davy's Gray; man, Cobalt Blue and Yellow Ochre.

136

WATER-COLOR, PASTEL,
AND CASEIN PAINTING;
BLACK AND WHITE;
PICTURE-MAKING HINTS

AN INTRODUCTION TO
WATER-COLOR PAINTING

Although water-color painting is many centuries old, its application as we know it today is fairly recent. Used in the past by the Egyptians on papyrus and by the Chinese on silk, it gradually evolved to become an important medium on paper. Its original use on paper was to elaborate upon line drawings with monochromatic washes. Color followed, with the line still used for drawing and modeling of form.

It was not until Winslow Homer appeared that water color became a medium to be handled directly on the spot in a broad manner. While these early water colors were used as a means of study from nature for subsequent oils, they came to have all the power contained in the heavier oil medium. Water color continues to be a medium that lends itself readily to painting on the spot, and working directly from nature is the most vital part of learning to handle it, aside from the original intention of studying the various aspects of nature. It is only after a long period of outdoor study that a reasonably convincing water color can be made in the studio.

If you have worked in oils, you will find the knowledge you have acquired in painting with this heavier medium very helpful in doing water colors. Experience in drawing and composition, and the training of your eye to see color, will all stand you in good stead. Now all you have to do is master the technique of handling water color!

To acquire this technique requires much practice. When working in oils you could finally arrive at the desired effect by much mixing of color, scraping the canvas for a fresh start, and making changes by the application of an opaque color over a previously painted area. Now you must work more directly. The beauty of water color lies in its fresh, transparent effect, and the approach must often be one in which the value, color, and drawing are accomplished in a single operation. However, while this is the ultimate effect you may want to achieve, a subject can be painted by separating these important ingredients into progressive stages.

The paper upon which you work is also a vital factor in imparting luminosity to a water-color painting, because the whiteness of the paper showing through the transparent color aids in establishing a brilliant effect.

The novice has a tendency to work with too small a brush on an equally small surface. I advise you to work with as large a brush as possible and to do your early work on a half sheet rather than a quarter sheet. This will help to prevent a niggling or timid approach; the larger brushes and working size will force you to work more broadly. Later, when you have acquired more technical facility, you can work on any size.

The demonstrations on pages 130-136 and 168-172 show an approach in which a preliminary drawing is always stressed. As you progress you will undoubtedly want to try other methods, possibly painting a subject directly with color or combining water color with other media. You will find that water color is an excellent medium for experimentation.

Sketch At All Times

MATERIAL AND EQUIPMENT
FOR WATER-COLOR PAINTING

Colors

If you have worked with oil colors, you should use the same selection of colors for your water-color palette. However, if you are starting directly with water color I recommend the following palette:

Alizarin Crimson
Cadmium Yellow, Light
Cadmium Red, Light
French Ultramarine
Ivory Black
Light Red
Thalo Green
Yellow Ochre

As you work you will find that adding the following colors is helpful in attaining many elusive shades difficult to mix with the limited list above.

Burnt Sienna
Burnt Umber
Chromium Oxide Green
Cobalt Blue
Davy's Gray
Paynes Gray
Thalo Blue
Cerulean Blue

Like oil colors, water colors are made in student and professional qualities. Besides being tubed, water colors are also available in pans. Both tube and pan colors are soluble in water, but the former are more popular. You can squeeze out the amount of color necessary for the painting on hand, thus insuring fresh color each time you paint.

Tube colors also allow the artist to mix large amounts of color washes in a much shorter time than do pan colors.

Accessories

The Easel

For indoor work you can use a table or a drawing board to support your water-color paper. Outdoors you can use an easel that has been designed for water-color painting. You can work at it sitting or standing, and it is adjustable to any angle. Or you may prefer to work with the water-color paper tacked to a small drawing board placed in your lap or on the ground.

Another way of working is to carry two small folding stools, one to sit on and the other to support the board. I prefer to travel as lightly as possible and generally paint seated with a water-color block on my lap. This works out very well, particularly on a sunny day, because you can sit in such a position that your body casts a shadow over the paper.

The Paint Box

Select a paint box that has generous-sized compartments in which to squeeze the paint. There are several kinds of boxes available. One model holds your tubes of paint and has a lid that can be used for a palette. You can arrange your colors in various ways. If the box has a double tray or compartment for the colors, one tray can be used for the cool colors and the other for the warm colors. You may, instead, want to arrange colors from light to dark.

Paper

The quality of paper that you use for water-color painting is most important. All-rag, hand-made paper is the best, but is fairly expensive and is becoming increasingly difficult to obtain. Many manufacturers are now producing a mold-made paper to take the place of the hand-made product. However, it is still all-rag and can take much rough handling and washing out of unwanted color.

The thickness of water-color paper is determined by the weight. Popular weights are 72-, 140-, 200-, and 300-pound, and the price increases with the weight. A 72-pound paper is rather thin but it can be used if you do not work too large. As the average sheet is 22 x 30 inches in all weights, I suggest that you quarter the sheet when using the 72-pound paper. The 140-pound weight is good for larger paintings (from one-half sheet upward) and the 200- and 300-pound weights are ideal for working on a full sheet of paper.

You can also obtain water-color paper mounted on stiff cardboard. This is an advantage in that the surface remains absolutely flat while you are painting.

Along with the various weights of paper, there are three different surfaces, rough, cold-pressed, and hot-pressed. The rough texture is best for your first ventures into water color. Cold-pressed paper, a smoother-textured surface that enables you to put in more detail, is the choice of many professional painters. Hot-pressed paper is considered too slick a surface for most water-colorists. I recommend the rough paper for your initial efforts, because it will take much more abuse and rubbing out than the smoother cold-pressed paper.

Preparing the Paper

The paper can be fastened to the drawing board, or any rigid support, in several ways. If it is heavy enough, a thumb tack or a heavy paper clip in each corner will hold the paper to the board with a minimum amount of buckling.

Lighter-weight paper can be attached to your drawing board with gummed tape. First wet the paper so that it becomes limp and rests flat on the board. Moisten the tape and apply it along the four sides of the paper, fastening it securely to the board; as the paper dries it will shrink, and when completely dry the surface will be tight and smooth. Have the board in a flat position at all times to insure the paper's drying evenly. Two-inch tape will securely hold the largest sheet of paper.

Another method of preparing a good working surface is to stretch the paper on canvas strips, a similar procedure to the one used in stretching canvas for oil painting. Select a set of strips the size you wish to work. Cut the paper with a margin of at least 1 inch around the four sides. Wet the paper thoroughly and then fasten it to the canvas stretcher with a thumb tack placed in the center of the outer edge of each side. Press thumb tacks on either side of the center tack, working toward the corners. The tacks should be placed a few inches apart, depending upon the size of the paper you are stretching. Allow the sheet to dry thoroughly in a horizontal position before starting to work.

Paper also comes made up in pads or blocks in various sizes. While the smaller blocks are handy for outdoor sketching, the paper in the larger sizes has a tendency to buckle when moistened.

There are some fairly good student brands of inexpensive water-color paper on the market, along with all-rag, machine-made paper. If you cannot afford the hand-made paper, I advise you to obtain as heavy a weight and as rough a texture as possible in the all-rag, machine-made paper. If you make many corrections your water color will lose its luster, but if you work as directly as possible, with a minimum amount of superimposed washes, good results can be achieved. Since paper plays such an important part in water colors, I think it is better to economize by using inexpensive student colors rather than use a cheaper paper.

Other Equipment

You will need a container in which to carry water when working outdoors. A bottle with a large cap will answer the purpose and the cap can be used as a water cup.

A small soft sponge will be found useful for wetting large areas quickly. Save paint rags to clean the palette and wipe your brushes.

All the equipment purchased for painting outdoors can be used in the studio. However, when working indoors it is more convenient to use two containers of water. Keep one for mixing colors and the other for cleaning brushes. You can also use a much larger palette, either a white china dish or a large white pan; paintings made in the studio are generally larger than those painted outdoors, so the larger palette will prove most welcome.

Brushes

Water-color brushes come in several grades. The best are the pure red sable, and, although they are expensive, they will last a long time if you take proper care of them. Cheaper brushes can be substituted, but a poor brush lacks the necessary spring and the point tends to spread in a short time.

Whatever type you select, I suggest that you obtain numbers 4, 8, and 12. These three brushes will answer the purpose for any size you choose to work in. A flat brush of single-stroke style, either $\frac{1}{2}$ or 1 inch wide, will be a useful supplement for the pointed brushes. It can be used for moistening the paper and laying large washes, and in straight painting.

Use a bristle brush for removing an unwanted passage of color. The stiffer hairs of this brush will remove the paint much faster than the softer sables and will save the latter from unnecessary wear.

Rinse your brushes thoroughly after using, squeezing out the surplus water by placing the hairs between your thumb and index finger. Reshape and place them upright in a container with the brush end up. An occasional washing with a mild soap and lukewarm water will help prolong their life. Make certain that all the soap is removed before storing brushes.

Sketch At All Times

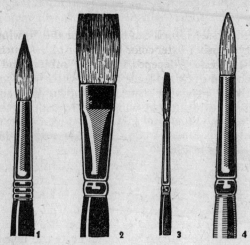

BRUSHES courtesy of M. Grumbacher, Inc., Mfr. of Brushes, Colors, Artists' Material

No. 1 Sable
Sable brushes will serve for most of your work.

No. 2 Flat
The 1-inch flat brush is useful for large areas and backgrounds. It will quickly moisten your paper if you prefer a preliminary wash of clear water preparatory to painting.

No. 3 Rigger
The rigger, with its chiseled edge, can depict the finest lines and sharp details.

No. 4 Round
The round bristle brush, while designed primarily for working in oil, is useful for removing unwanted areas of water color.

THE DRAWING

A medium-soft pencil can be used for the drawing preparatory to using water-color paints. Just how much penciling is necessary depends upon the subject and your experience in drawing. Some artists use charcoal to indicate only the general proportions of the subject, and complete the drawing as they paint. Others dispense entirely with a preliminary drawing and work directly with paint.

I advise you to make a fairly comprehensive drawing in the beginning, but take care not to erase any more than necessary. The surface of the paper is easily injured by erasing, and painting over such an area will cause the paint to go on unevenly. Use a soft-soap or a kneaded eraser, taking care in the case of the latter that no grease from your fingers is transmitted to the paper. Do not attempt to shade with the pencil but do indicate the division of light and shadow by line.

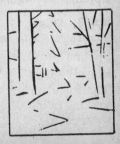

A more detailed drawing is made when the subject is more involved, as shown above. A rough indication is enough for a simple subject.

HANDLING WATER COLOR

The inexperienced student often grasps the water-color brush like a pencil, completing the entire painting without varying his grip on the ferrule. While the brush should be held in this position for strong decisive strokes, you should practice gripping it everywhere from the base of the ferrule to the tip of the wooden handle. Notice how your stroke varies from a heavy blob to a fine hairline, and practice this brush handling on scraps of paper or on the back of discarded water-color paintings. Learn how to apply a flat even wash, a wash from light to dark, and one from dark to light. It is only through much practice that you will learn how to control various washes. Try tilting the board while doing a graded wash. In some instances you will tilt the board toward you, in others, away from you. Do not have the board at too acute an angle, or the wash will dry unevenly; 15 degrees should be enough.

In the beginning your washes will probably be weak. You will discover that certain colors will spread more evenly than others. Paints with much staining quality, such as Alizarin Crimson, are difficult to lay evenly. Others have a heavy sediment which appears as the wash dries, yet the effect is not unpleasant. Indeed, this effect can be used to advantage when certain textures are desired. Make notes of how various colors react when made soluble with water. You will find that some become pale or lighter almost immediately while others, with greater covering power, hold on to the original color tenaciously.

Blend one color, while it is still wet, into another, then add a third color to the mixture. You will soon find that a muddy effect results when too many colors are mixed together. However, in all these exercises you will discover beautiful grays and pleasing color combinations. Along with the mixing of wet colors, make several flat washes, each of a separate color. Allow to dry and then paint another color over the previously painted wash. Note how the under-color affects the second wash. Try not to drag your strokes when applying one color over another, else you may disturb the under-color. Work quickly and directly, using a full brush.

When you start painting your subject, you will find that:

1. Water-color paint should be applied at a darker or stronger intensity than oil paint, because it dries lighter. This is particularly true when working outdoors on a bright, sunny day.

2. A direct manner and a full brush are necessary to achieve the luminosity that is so important in a water color.

3. You should always mix more of a color wash than you think you will need.

4. The paper is important in creating the sparkling effect that typifies water-color painting.

LINE COMBINED WITH WATER COLOR

You can achieve pleasing effects by combining a line drawing with water color. The most popular approach is to outline the subject with black India ink. You can use a pen or a brush, but with the latter you will more easily obtain a flexible and varying line. Do not make a hard, detailed ink rendering of the subject. Instead, attempt to have a "lost-and-found" line with occasional heavier accents. Using a pointed brush instead of a pen will help to avoid giving the rendering a stiff, rigid look and will enable you to obtain either a thick or a thin line.

When the ink is dry, you begin to paint as you would when doing a regular water color. Sparkling effects are achieved by not slavishly filling in the inked outline but by applying the color freely, missing the outline at times and overlapping the lines occasionally. The inked drawing will keep the subject recognizable at all times.

A preliminary line drawing is especially helpful for architectural subjects. Then a tighter rendering can be made to insure that all of the necessary details are depicted. When doing such a subject, it is a good idea to use a pen.

Different-colored inks can be used for experimenting with this technique. They may not be absolutely water-proof, but occasional blurring or running of the line can add charm to the water color. A sepia-colored ink is often more harmonious than black, and you might mix black and red ink to obtain an interesting-colored outline.

A water color that has turned out to be unsuccessful because of a weak over-all effect can often be salvaged by line work. The weak areas are generally caused by faulty values, which result in their being lost in the picture. By outlining the entire painting the over-all effect is immediately strengthened. Experiment with your discarded water colors—you will be surprised how many can be made at least presentable.

Sketch At All Times

The line drawing.

The completed water color.

DEVELOPING THE OUTDOOR SKETCH
INTO A STUDIO WATER COLOR

After you have worked directly from nature for some time, you may want to develop some of your sketches into larger paintings. You will do most of your on-the-spot work on one-quarter and one-half sheets, but it is good practice to paint on a full sheet occasionally.

I advise you to restrict your early large water-color efforts to the studio. You can work in a more leisurely manner, and the convenience of plenty of water, large mixing trays, and extra equipment allows you to concentrate on the difficult task of transferring your sketch to a more ambitious studio painting.

Use at least a 140-pound paper—the heavier the better—when working full size. The texture can be rough or cold-pressed, depending upon the subject matter and your personal preference. Keep in mind that rough paper will take more handling and working over than smoother paper.

With your original sketch before you, start to redraw the subject on the large sheet. Do not hesitate to make any changes that you think will help strengthen the composition. Put in all the detail you feel is necessary, so that when you start to paint you can concentrate on the various color passages.

Since most water-color palettes or trays have only small wells to hold your mixed color, I suggest that you use some old saucers for mixing large washes—and again, always mix more color than you think you will use. Running short of mixed color just before a wash is completed always seems to be a student's chief difficulty, and it is almost impossible to match an incompleted wash that has dried.

The discussion on page 219 of the difficulty of painting a large picture applies equally to water color. Certain passages of color that look acceptable in the sketch often lose something when they are enlarged. A suggestive bit of color in the sketch has to be painted as a more definite statement in the larger picture.

The same goes for your drawing. A pleasing blob of color may pass for a cow in a small sketch, but some knowledge of its anatomy must be revealed when it is painted on a larger scale.

If you encounter too much difficulty working on a full sheet, a more gradual working up to a larger size may be advisable. You could do your early studio painting the same size as your sketch, and follow up by working possibly a third larger, then double the size, until you have attained technical competence. Then try the full-sized sheet again.

Have on hand a mat with an opening that corresponds to the size of the water color you are painting, and place it over the water color from time to time. This will give you a fresh view of the subject as well as a check on how much further to carry the painting.

Above all, try to give your studio paintings all the fresh spontaneity of an outdoor sketch.

WATER-COLOR-PAINTING HINTS

If your water color is off in value, especially if the darks are too dark, you can use opaque or casein color to correct them. The dark passages can easily be lightened, but the charm of transparent water-color is lost.

I suggest that you use the unsuccessful sketch as a basis for reference. Redraw the composition in the studio and repaint the subject. Try to do this as soon as you can, while your impression of the subject is still fresh. You may be pleasantly surprised to find that your studio painting of the subject has a more "outdoor" look to it than the one made on the spot. After all, you observed the subject directly from nature for several hours, and even though the spot sketch was unsuccessful you salvaged your mental observations of the subject.

Use a dry brush to lift the excess color as a wash is completed. This blob of excess color invariably forms when a fully saturated wash is applied. If not removed it will dry darker than the rest of the painted area.

To lighten a painted area on rough paper use a hard eraser or a piece of fine sandpaper. This method, used judiciously, will often give life to an area that has become deadened because of too many washes of color.

There is a water-color varnish that brightens areas that have become dull through excessive rubbing out and correcting. It dries with a sheen, but if it is used sparingly it is not very noticeable when framed behind glass.

Blocking-Out Methods

As you work with water color the problem of retaining light, intricate shapes that are surrounded by strong darks will arise. Many times it is almost impossible to paint around these light shapes, particularly if they are small. Block out these shapes with a thin solution of rubber cement and a small brush before any paint is applied. When the cement is dry, paint the dark areas, letting the color cover the rubber cement. When the paint is thoroughly dry, remove the cement by rubbing it lightly with your finger. The untouched white paper will be revealed and you can paint it whatever color you wish. A commercial solution known as Maskoid is made expressly for this purpose and is easy to handle. If you are working on a full sheet of paper and the area to be covered is correspondingly large, you can use masking tape cut to the shape to be blocked out.

Use of a Razor Blade

A razor blade or a knife can be used to scrape sharp white lines or small shapes from a water-color painting. Telephone wires, branches of a white birch tree, seagulls in flight, are some examples of things that can be scraped from the painted surface. These implements are also useful for obtaining textural effects on casein painted on a gesso board.

Using a Wet Blotter to Retard Drying

Place on your drawing board a wet blotter the size of the paper upon which you are going to work, and tack your paper over the blotter after the pencil drawing is made. The wet blotter underneath will enable you to work and blend color on a damp surface for a much longer period. By substituting a sheet of glass, metal, or any flat nonporous material for the wood drawing board, you can keep the wet blotter moist even longer.

Angle of the Board

Do not tilt the board supporting your water color at too acute an angle when laying a color wash over a large area. Tilt the board just enough to keep the color flowing. Too much of an angle will cause the wash to dry unevenly.

Allowing for Contrast

Painting colors strongly, to allow for lightening when the water color dries, is particularly important when you are starting the painting, for the surrounding white paper makes the color appear darker in comparison.

Use of the Sponge

A small sponge will be found useful for wetting the paper quickly and for covering tonal washes of color. It can also be used to sponge out cloud forms. The sky area is painted, and before drying the sponge is moistened with clean water. The cloud formation is shaped by wiping the wet sky color from the paper. Unwanted passages of color can also be removed with a sponge.

For More Luminosity

When painting a mass area, first apply the dominating color. Then, while the area is still wet, work other color into it. Far more luminosity and richer color is added to the painting through this method.

Strength Through Dry Brush

A way of strengthening the water color is to use a dry-brush technique over parts of the painting that lend themselves to it. Foreground, foliage, and some of the shaded areas can be intensified with this technique.

Various-Sized Mats As a Picture Aid

Have mats of various sizes on hand when reviewing the results of your summer's output of water colors. Some of the more doubtful sketches may be improved by matting out a poorly painted area, and some that are already matted may be improved by rematting. Even pictures you consider hopeless may contain areas that suggest interesting compositions for future studio paintings.

You may also wish to experiment with toned mats. For example, a pearl-gray mat will enhance a water color in which a considerable amount of the original white paper remains as part of the design. These white areas appear more intense, more sparkling, when surrounded by the gray mat.

Absorbent Paper Tissues

Absorbent tissues can be used for picking up blobs of excess wet color. If it is slightly moistened with clean water, the tissue can be molded into a tapering shape, to make it much handier than a sponge for removing a small amount of color.

Spattering for Textural Effect

An old toothbrush or a stiff bristle brush can be used for spatter effects. The brush is dipped into the color and a match or a penknife is pulled over the hairs. When it is used judiciously, spattering creates interesting effects. It can be done with varying effects over both wet and dry areas. Take precautions to block off with newspaper the area of your water color where spattered color is not wanted.

STUDIO SKETCHES FROM MEMORY

After you have completed a day's work of painting on the spot, try repainting the subject from memory the following day. It should still be fresh enough in your mind's eye for you to be able to paint a quick impression of the scene. This is an excellent exercise in developing your powers of observation and you may be pleasantly surprised with the results. You need not necessarily try a large painting—several small sketches will do. Omit the drawing and concentrate on the color as you remember it, applying it directly with the brush.

The "Quickie" Water Color

A variation of the exercise suggested above is a water color done in five or ten minutes. The subject can be from memory or improvised, realistic or abstract. The important thing is to finish the painting in a short space of time.

Excellent sizes of paper for this exercise are 8 x 10 and 9 x 12 inches. You can use the backs of discarded water colors, cutting them down to size.

Work directly with the brush, omitting the usual preliminary pencil drawing. By working rapidly you will learn much about the handling of water color in a spontaneous manner. Vary your approach—sometimes do a series of sketches in a wet technique, at other times use a dry-brush technique.

WATER-COLOR-PAINTING DEMONSTRATIONS

The three demonstrations on pages 130-136 illustrate several approaches to painting a water color. They are planned to enable you to keep the medium under control at all times. An effective way to do that is shown in the first demonstration. This method is based on the early English school of water-color painting: applying light color washes first, then working to the darker areas, and gradually arriving at the desired tones.

In the United States we have developed a more direct approach. Some of the leading water-colorists reverse the English method by starting with the dark areas first and working the lighter colors around these areas.

The first demonstration, the Lone House, illustrates an approach in which the center of interest is painted first and the sky in the latter stages. This can be done when the shape against the sky is a simple one, for then the laying of the sky color around it is not too difficult. However, when there are several shapes against the sky it is better to paint the latter first and the shapes over it. The Red Barn is an example of this procedure.

Another method is shown in Maine Boatman. Here the value ranges from light to dark and is established early by painting the sky area and then the dark foreground. The rest of the subject is painted in between these values.

The demonstration on page 168, Winter House, shows still another approach. The shadow areas form an interesting design and are painted first. A pattern is immediately formed which reveals the distribution of the light and dark areas, suggesting the picture almost from the start.

Try all these methods; from your experiments you will develop your own style.

AN INTRODUCTION TO PASTEL PAINTING

The medium of pastel is represented by very few entries in contemporary art exhibitions. The difficulty of fixing pastel has undoubtedly contributed to its decline in popularity. Pastel paintings can be sprayed with a special fixatif at preliminary stages to keep them from smearing, but the final stage must be left unfixed if its delicate color is to be held. This means that pastels must always be carefully framed under glass in order to preserve them. Actually, the glass is necessary to protect the surface of the pastel rather than to preserve it, for, as a medium, pastel will outlast both water color and oil.

Pastel is popular with many portrait and figure painters, as a means of making both preliminary studies and final renderings, and the student of landscape will find pastels helpful in capturing passing effects, particularly clouds and skies. It is an excellent medium for quick notes on nocturnes, water reflections, and sunlight effects.

Many artists use pastel for making sketches and studies preliminary to painting in oil. Since it is a dry medium, changes are made easily and quickly.

The color of the paper used when working with pastel is often left untouched in many areas, particularly in backgrounds. This, along with a direct handling method that reveals all the strokes of the modeling, has led many students to think of pastel as a drawing rather than a painting medium. However, pastel can be applied in such a manner that all the paper is covered and a painting effect results. Despite its present lack of popularity, I suggest that you experiment with pastel. It has great possibilities and you may make the pleasant discovery that pastel is ideally suited for recording ideas that may become important oil and water-color paintings.

EQUIPMENT FOR PASTEL PAINTING

While a limited palette of color can be used when working with oil or water color, a much larger assortment of colors is needed for pastels. The various grays, which are so important to the outdoor painter, are always mixed by the oil painter and water-colorist, but in pastel these vital shades are already prepared and a full assortment of grayed colors should be included.

Pastels come in sets of various sizes, from boxes of forty sticks to an elaborate chest of drawers containing over four hundred. Select a box containing at least sixty pastels to insure a range of colors for different color schemes.

Drawing Board

Your regular drawing board can be used when working with pastel. Some newspaper or extra sheets of pastel paper should be placed under the paper you are using to create a softer and somewhat yielding surface.

Paper

Pastel paper is obtainable in various colors. You can use charcoal paper or any paper that possesses a grained, textural surface to which the pastel can adhere. Do not keep your paper rolled; store it flat instead.

Rags and Chamois

Keep a soft rag handy for pastel areas that may have to be lightly rubbed down or wiped off. A chamois can be used for partially removing too heavy an accumulation of pastel. It is also useful for blending and smoothing colors.

Charcoal

Charcoal sticks can be used for the preliminary drawing, especially when the subject is a landscape. Details and accents can also be rendered with charcoal.

Portfolio

A portfolio is convenient for carrying pastel paper and acts as a sketching support when you are working outdoors. Have a few sheets of smooth tracing paper to put over your sketches when they are finished. Place the covered sketches carefully in the portfolio and tie it securely so that there can be no movement.

Fixatif

There are especially prepared pastel fixatifs available but at best they are not too successful. Since a pastel should not be fixed at its final stage, any of the delicate colors that are added at this time are best preserved under glass. However, if you do wish to fix the pastel at its completion, do not spray it too heavily. Spray it lightly a few times, allowing a drying interval between each fixing.

Stumps

Paper stumps come in various sizes and can be used for fine blending. Use them sparingly, because an unpleasant slick effect will result if they are used too generously.

WORKING WITH PASTELS

Pastels are available in hard, semi-hard, and soft, with the latter preferred by most artists. They are all fragile and break easily no matter how carefully you handle them, but this should not cause much concern, for work is seldom done with a full-sized pastel stick. A small piece affords more flexibility in handling; it can be used on its side for broad effects, and the tip is fine for details.

Because the set remains unbroken for so short a time, care should be taken to keep the colors in sequence. Then, when you have finished working with a broken piece, place it back in its original order.

On the following page are shown three progressive stages in the use of pastel when doing a portrait. The first stage shows the necessary outline before actual color is applied. In this demonstration a light cream paper is used and the head and its planes are roughly indicated with Light Red pastel.

The next step is to fill in the shaded area indicated in the outline. The same Light Red can be used, since it roughly corresponds with the shaded flesh tones. The area is filled in with the side of the pastel, resulting in a broad effect. At the conclusion of this stage a rough indication of the distribution of the light and shadow areas is revealed. The light area is represented by the original cream paper.

The third stage shows the head modeled completely with color. The original rough indication of shadow has been rubbed into the paper. Then, with this tone as a guide, the pastel has been applied in a direct manner. Strokes of warm and cool color are placed side by side and in some areas cross-hatched with a neutral color. Rubbing in of color is kept to a minimum, for the vibrant quality of pastel is best expressed with short, direct strokes.

THE THREE PRINCIPAL STEPS IN MAKING A PASTEL PORTRAIT

Above: the outline is made, using a warm-tone pastel.

Left: The shadow area is roughly indicated, using a pastel stick of its approximate flesh tone.

Right: The shadow area is rubbed down with the fingers and the various colors are applied in short, direct strokes.

USING PASTEL FOR QUICK FIGURE SKETCHING

Pastel is an excellent medium for quick, crisp color rendering of the figure. It is particularly effective for figures in brightly colored costumes. The various textures, from light and shining to heavy and dull material, can be rendered quickly.

Below is shown a fifteen-minute sketch from the model. Charcoal on a gray paper was used to indicate the pose of the figure and the main lines of her costume. Color followed, applied with the flat side of the pastel.

A red conté pencil, as a preparation for pastel, is excellent when outlining a nude figure. The warm red blends nicely with the subsequent layer of pastel.

The pose of the model is indicated with a few simple lines on a gray-toned paper.

Pastel color is quickly applied. This is a typical fifteen-minute sketch.

LANDSCAPE NOTES WITH PASTEL

Making landscape color notes with pastel has many advantages. All you need is a pad and a small box of pastels, instead of the more cumbersome equipment needed when working with oils or even with water color or casein.

The pad you use for pastel landscape work should preferably be of a tinted paper. Such pads are available and can be obtained with a variety of tints within a single pad. When sketching outdoors you can choose a color that is harmonious with the subject. The simplest procedure is not to attempt to cover an entire area of the paper but to allow the paper itself to be part of the design.

The illustration above shows a quick sketch rendered on a gray paper. As you can see, quite a bit of the original paper is uncovered, but there are enough vital color notes to serve as references for a future studio painting.

PASTEL HINTS

• Pastel can be combined with water color, with the latter serving as an underpainting. Flat or slightly graded washes indicating the main areas of the subject can be rendered in water color on toned or white paper, and pastel then used in a direct manner until the picture is completed.

• By using pastels in just the dark areas of the picture at the start, the general pattern of light and shade is immediately achieved.

• If you use your fingers and thumb as an aid in blending colors, be sure they are free from grease. Try not to handle the kneaded eraser any more than necessary, as its oily content will soon leave a greasy film on your fingers.

• A resilient and sympathetic working surface can be obtained by tacking pastel paper over a stretched canvas.

• A sheet of water-color paper can be tinted with a colored wash preparatory to working over it in pastel.

• Black emery paper will receive pastel very well. It is an excellent background for making notes of sunlight breaking through wooded or forest subjects.

• Passages that have gone dull or are too dark in a water-color painting can be given life and lightened by a few discreet touches of pastel. Care must be employed not to make this correcting device too obvious.

• Heavy brown wrapping paper can be used as a substitute for the more expensive pastel paper. It possesses a good working surface and the brown color makes an excellent background. Fine sandpaper is another surface that will receive pastel very well.

WATER-COLOR DEMONSTRATION

Winter House

The first water-color demonstration (page 130) was painted with a limited selection of colors, eight in all.

In this demonstration an even more restricted palette is used. The entire painting is done with Yellow Ochre, Light Red, and Cobalt Blue. By mixing these three colors in various combinations all the other shades of color will be obtained. You will be surprised at the number of colors that can be mixed with so limited a palette. Actually, the three colors used correspond roughly to the primary colors. The Yellow Ochre and the Light Red are neutralized yellow and red primaries; Cobalt Blue is fairly close to the primary blue.

In discovering the variety of colors that can be produced by so restricted a palette, you at the same time become aware of the harmonious effect that can be achieved. This realization will bear out the statement made in Color-Mixing Exercises (pages 37-38) that the fewer colors used in mixing, the easier it is to obtain color harmony.

The usual pencil drawing is made of the subject.

A wash of Cobalt Blue is applied over the shaded areas. A Yellow Ochre wash is then painted over the sky and window shades, followed by Light Red for the chimneys. The green of the door and shutters is a mixture of Yellow Ochre and Cobalt Blue. The sky is moistened with clear water and some Cobalt Blue floated into the upper area.

The painting continues with a mixture of Yellow Ochre and Light Red for the foliage. The green distant hills and the smaller house are then painted with Yellow Ochre and Cobalt Blue. A mixture of Light Red and Cobalt Blue is used for the bare trees.

The details are now rendered, still with only the three original colors. The darkest accents are made by mixing Cobalt Blue and Light Red at their fullest strength, with just enough water added to make the mixture workable.

AN INTRODUCTION TO CASEIN PAINTING

Many artists are now adding the medium of casein to water color and oil, and you will probably enjoy working with it. A flexible, permanent medium, it is easy to handle and requires no reorientation in color mixing, since the same pigments are used as in the other two media. Since casein is soluble in water and is frequently used on paper, where it dries quickly with a matte-like effect, a casein painting resembles a water color when completed. When handled in a similar manner, but painted on a rigid surface such as gesso board, it can be varnished when finished and will then take on the appearance of an oil painting.

Placed in heavy, close-fitting frames, varnished caseins are often entered in oil exhibitions and are most difficult to distinguish from oil paintings.

Many artists use casein as a base or underpainting and then finish the painting with oil glazes. Great luminosity is achieved this way. It is important to remember, however, that a coating of casein varnish must be brushed over the casein base before oil glazing is begun. Otherwise the oil paint will sink into the casein base and a dulling of the color will eventually take place. I also advise you not to repaint with casein color after the varnish has been applied, because it may flake or chip off.

Some color manufacturers state that regular retouch varnish can be used to varnish casein paintings, but I think it is better to use a special casein varnish that is available in art supply shops.

The only medium necessary for casein color is water. Any type of brush can be used, but if you have worked in water color you will probably prefer a soft brush. Always wash the brushes immediately after use, for once the casein becomes imbedded in the hairs it is almost impossible to remove. A good idea is to have two jars of water, as you do for water-color work. One can be used for mixing and the other for keeping the brushes clean.

Any surface that is absorbent can be used. Water-color paper, illustration board, kid-finished bristol board, colored charcoal paper, and gesso board are all excellent. An especially prepared casein canvas can be obtained, but you can use any absorbent canvas that is not too heavily primed.

A sufficient range of colors is available to enable you to select your favorites.

Your first impression of this medium will be of its fast-drying quality. If this disturbs you, obtain a bottle of casein medium, which is mixed with water and the color.

Casein-painting demonstrations are on pages 204-209.

Casein As a Water Color

The simplest and most direct way of becoming familiar with casein is to use it in a manner similar to water color. Make your usual pencil drawing on a sheet of water-color paper, then squeeze the amount of color from the tube of casein that you would normally use for water color. Proceed to paint by diluting the casein with water, working in a transparent manner. You will immediately discover that caseins merge, blend, and dry similarly to water colors. One important difference is that a casein painting gradually becomes impervious to water after it is completed.

Casein As a Gouache

By reducing the amount of water used, an opaque effect
can be had with casein. By adding white, more solidity can
be achieved. Casein should not be applied too heavily at
one time; rather, build up weight and opacity through successive thinly painted layers. An advantage casein colors
have over the regular gouache colors is that they lose little
of their intensity when drying; the darks lose hardly any.
Along with using water-color paper, try painting on gesso
boards and toned papers. You will be amazed at the covering power of casein on the latter, no matter how dark the
tone. Try designing your composition so that some areas
of the toned paper remain untouched and form part of
the design of the picture, as on the following two pages.

Casein As an Underpainting for Oil

Casein makes an excellent underpainting for an oil
painting. Keep the underpainting on the light side, depending upon the oil glazes to give the full color. Varnish
the surface as before, to isolate the casein base. When the
varnish is dry, use your oil colors (see page 208). You can
work with oil in any way you wish, but rich luminosity is
best achieved by glazing. Use your copal painting medium
to cut the oil color to the transparent consistency you desire, and apply the color with a soft sable brush. Keeping in
mind that you will not achieve the color you want with the
initial glaze, paint a series of glazes until you reach the
depth of tone and color you are seeking. Each glaze should
be allowed to dry before another is applied over it. When
completed, the picture is treated as an oil painting and
can be given a coat of retouch varnish followed by a final
varnishing a few months later.

WORKING WITH CASEIN DIRECTLY OVER
YOUR ON-THE-SPOT SKETCHES

You may find it easier to complete a casein painting in the studio if you work from penciled color notations. Write your color notes over the various areas of your on-the-spot sketch as shown below.

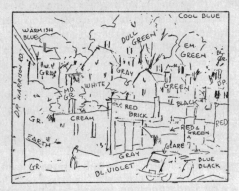

Study your notations back in the studio. Then, as the various colors are mixed, apply them directly over the noted areas. By painting opaquely, you can gradually cover the penciled notes with the results illustrated below.

Below is shown the outdoor sketch, made with black India ink applied with a brush.

The ink dries rapidly, allowing you to work with casein paint directly over the inked base. The black undertone serves to establish an arrangement of the light and dark areas. Interesting color effects are achieved by applying the casein thinly in some areas and more opaquely in others.

CASEIN PAINTING HINTS

• Heavier-painted casein areas become less absorbent and the first coat of varnish dries with more of a gloss than over the thinner, more absorbent areas. When casein has been applied with varying degrees of thickness, it may be necessary to use several coats of casein varnish to produce an even gloss on a painted surface. If you varnish the painting the first time with horizontal strokes, use vertical strokes for the second application.

• Its great absorbent quality frequently makes casein paint useful with other techniques in other media. For example, a coating of casein white over a sheet of rough paper makes an excellent surface for dry-brush rendering.

• A plastic spray will provide a glossy, protective coating on a finished casein painting. Place the painting in a vertical position and use a side-to-side motion, holding the spray about 12 inches away from the painted surface. Plastic spray should not be used if you intend to work with oil colors over the casein, because its ingredients are not compatible with oil.

• After a casein painting has been allowed to dry long enough to become waterproof (about thirty days), a series of transparent casein color washes can be applied. These washes can be built up in a manner similar to the glazing of an oil painting, and a delicate luminosity can be attained by alternating washes of warm and cool color.

• Copal painting medium will impart the highest gloss and greatest luminosity when used with oil color for glazing over an isolated casein painting.

• There is a casein painting medium available that will fortify the adhesive quality of highly diluted color. In large areas where the color has been excessively thinned with water, a small amount can be used to restore any binding strength that may have been lost and to give a semi-gloss to the casein color. In classes in which students work on a project for some time, casein mixtures should be stored in air-tight jars.

• Because casein colors are lime-proof, they can be used for painting murals on either wet or dry plaster walls. Casein varnish can be applied over the finished mural for temporary protection, and it will not have much effect on the matte finish that is usually desirable in a mural, because the plaster surface and the casein together have a tremendous amount of absorbency. If a slight gloss is not objectionable, regular copal or dammar varnish can be used on top of the casein varnish.

• Since fixatif is water-repellent, it should not be used over pencil or charcoal drawings preparatory to working with casein.

• Thinned casein color can be used in an airbrush, but be sure to clean the gun thoroughly immediately after using it.

• If you make your pencil sketch on the spot, using a good-quality paper, you can finish it in casein color at a later date. Make color notations in pencil on the various areas of the sketch, and later, in the studio, you can paint directly over it with casein, checking the penciled notes before applying the colors. When the casein is used in a gouache style, the notes are gradually opaqued out.

• Common heavy brown wrapping paper and black photograph-album sheets provide an inexpensive toned base for color sketches. The strong covering power of casein paint works to advantage on such a surface. Brown wrapping paper, which is available in rolls, is especially useful for working out the rough planning of large murals.

SIX BASIC RULES FOR USING CASEIN PAINT

1. Always add some water to the color.

2. Use an absorbent base to insure that the casein color adheres to the surface.

3. Do not apply the color too thickly, as it may chip or flake off.

4. You must isolate the casein surface with casein varnish before you begin to use oil on the painting.

5. Never allow brushes to dry with casein on them.

6. Wash brushes with soap and water.

AN INTRODUCTION TO BLACK AND WHITE

Black and white, whether rendered with pencil or brush, is the most convenient medium for sketching. All the equipment you need to carry, aside from a pencil or a pen, is a sketch pad.

For general landscape sketching a medium-soft pencil can be used. All the necessary shading can be accomplished by using the pencil on a fairly smooth paper.

I suggest that you work on a 9-x-12-inch pad. This size will allow you to produce anything from a small 2-x-3-inch compositional note to a detailed study on the full sheet. By using a smooth paper you can work faster, delineate fine details, and obtain broad, velvety black effects. In addition, you will find the smooth-surfaced paper more receptive to pen and ink.

The 9-x-12 pad is recommended for recording landscape compositions, impressions, and studies, and a smaller pad that can be conveniently slipped into the pocket and carried at all times is useful for sketching figures. By figures I mean people at work, at play, walking, sitting, and so on. This type of sketching serves two purposes: first, the constant practice will improve your drawing; second, the figures can often be incorporated into your paintings. However incidental they may be in your painting, they will lend an authoritative note if they were originally sketched from life.

For drawing the figure in the classroom or studio, charcoal is undoubtedly the best medium for serious study. The fact that charcoal has to be sprayed with a fixatif to keep it from smearing does not make it as satisfactory a sketching medium as pencil or pen.

The following pages describe various methods of using black and white.

PEN AND INK

There are many types of nibs available today, ranging from a delicate hairline to a broad, heavy line. For outdoor sketching it is awkward to carry a bottle of ink and often more difficult to find a flat area on which to rest it, so I suggest that you acquire a fountain pen with a stub or a flexible point that will enable you to draw boldly.

Fine point.   Stub point.

There are fountain pens specifically made for use with heavy black India ink, but an ordinary fountain pen with a deep blue-black ink will serve your purpose. It is only when you want to supplement the pen drawing with colored water-color washes that you encounter difficulty, because ordinary fountain-pen ink is water-soluble and will run, while India ink is waterproof. But even this disadvantage is turned into an advantage by many artists, who prefer the blurred line as being more "atmospheric."

You will find the pen most helpful in making small, quick sketches of figures. These sketches can be made in a small notebook that can be carried conveniently in the pocket or purse.

File these notebooks for future use—you will often find a pose in them that will fit into a picture you are composing in the studio.

EXAMPLES OF PEN AND INK

Architectural subjects can be either tightly or loosely rendered with the pen.

A subject in a strong light can be quickly captured by rendering the shadow areas with all the pen lines going in the same direction.

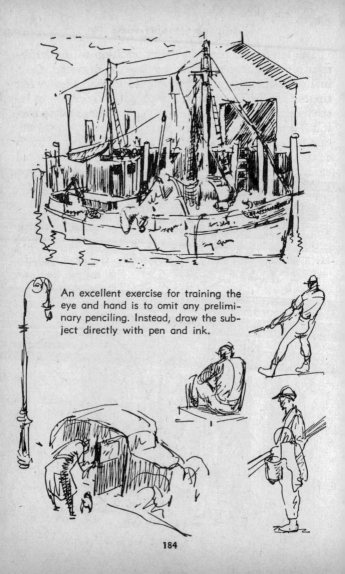

An excellent exercise for training the eye and hand is to omit any preliminary penciling. Instead, draw the subject directly with pen and ink.

184

THE FELT-TIPPED PEN

The felt-tipped pen is a recent addition to the implements used in rendering black and white drawings. Originally designed as a marking instrument with a heavy felt tip, the pen has been streamlined. With a selection of interchangeable nibs available in various sizes and shapes, it has become a popular sketching tool. Similar to a fountain pen, it contains a reservoir of ink. The flow of ink is controlled and the line can be varied from a bold, broad effect to a thin, pencil-like stroke. It is my favorite drawing tool and many of the illustrations in this book were made with it.

The felt-tipped pen is excellent for quick sketching, and dry-brush as well as tonal effects can be obtained by using paper with a slight tooth to it. Several colored inks are available but I find black and brown the most useful.

USING THE FELT-TIPPED PEN

Subjects requiring
strong shadows are
excellently rendered
with the felt pen.

A brief, casual pose is
captured as the felt
pen quickly glides over
a smooth-surfaced
paper.

Tonal contrasts can also be accomplished. A rough-surfaced paper
is recommended for such work as an aid in controlling the light and
dark tones.

THE BRUSH

Using the brush to sketch directly from nature is not as convenient as using a pencil or a fountain pen, for a bottle of ink or a tube of paint must be carried, and if paint is used, a container of water and a small mixing tray are necessary.

I have found that it is usually worthwhile to carry the extra equipment in order to obtain preliminary sketches that can be carried further along in color upon returning to the studio. The sketch on page 191 is an excellent example. The drawing was made on the spot, using black ink, with some areas of the sketch rendered lighter by diluting the ink with water. A tonal effect was thus achieved and served as a painting base for the color, which was applied in the studio.

Using the brush on the paper without a preliminary penciled composition is also excellent practice for direct handling. The eye must carefully survey the subject and the mind determine just what is to be depicted before the brush touches the paper. A number 4 pointed sable brush will answer the purpose for most types of sketching. Make certain that the brush is thoroughly washed when you finish, for black India ink shortens the life of sable hairs.

THREE STEPS IN USING THE BRUSH FOR SKETCHING

Step 1

A light pencil indication is made of the main lines of the composition. Then, using ink or black water color, the general outline of the subject is made.

Step 2

The shading begins with brushing-in of the largest areas.

Step 3

The rest of the darks follow and the sketch is completed when the details are rendered.

HOW TO USE BLACK AND WHITE NOTES
FOR PAINTING

Black and white notes can be successfully used in the studio only after much time is spent painting directly from nature.

Many color studies must be made on the spot, with observation of the color relationship of one element to another, the atmospheric values, and the constantly changing moods of nature. Color knowledge is acquired only after long study and there is no short cut possible at this stage of your painting career.

The following pages illustrate a few methods that can be applied when you are ready to work from black and white notes. The most common method is that shown on page 190, in which a drawing is made of the subject and the colors are written in the various areas. These color notations can be as elaborate as you wish, depending on the complexity of the subject. It is good practice to paint the subject in your studio as soon as possible. You will then still retain a visual impression of the scene that, supplemented with your notes, will give you a better chance of turning out a successful painting.

There is no doubt that we see many subjects in which the color effect is too fleeting, even if we had our painting equipment available. This is where the use of a quick pencil sketch, with color notations, is the only means of capturing the effect.

As you use penciled notes you will undoubtedly frequently improvise your own color in areas that you feel

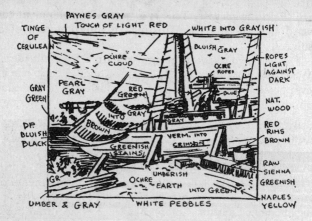

Color notations are made on the sketch and the margin.

Even the most fragmentary sketch can possess possibilities for a future studio painting. This quick sketch was made from a train window.

will help the picture. This is a natural development toward creating your own distinctive interpretation of a subject.

However, you have to return to nature for fresh ideas. When you work in full color—and you should do so whenever possible—you will be pleasantly surprised to find that you have not painted quite all that nature has to offer.

Some subjects are difficult to paint on the spot because of weather conditions, and consequently have to be done from sketches. The sketch above was made with black ink on a white illustration board, with the ink diluted in areas where I wanted to show a tonal change. A composition showing the light and dark pattern resulted. Later, in the studio, I painted directly over the black ink with casein colors. One of the chief advantages of using casein is that its powerful covering quality takes it over the black passages with ease, completely obliterating the ink wherever desired. In some areas I applied the casein thinly, to allow the ink to show through where it helped the effect.

PICTURE-MAKING HINTS

Once the student has acquired the necessary technique to interpret his ideas, he should find picture-making relatively easy. Actually, as progress is made, the student realizes that technique is secondary—that *design* or *composition* is most important. Picture-making essentially is the *design* of an idea. While certain fundamental rules can be followed, such as not placing the object of interest too close to the edge of the picture, the student must work out his own compositional problems.

There is no infallible formula. The following hints, however, comprise the more obvious "do's and don'ts" of picture-making.

The distance between yourself and the subject you are sketching may vary. Generally you should be where your eyes can take in all of the subject that is to appear in your composition without your having to turn left or right. It is frequently difficult for the beginner to determine just where the foreground should start. While it should not include the immediate area in which you are standing, neither should it begin so far away that your object of interest is dwarfed. About twelve feet from where you stand is the minimum distance to form the base of your picture.

Actually, the problem should be solved in terms of what you are attempting to convey. If it is a sunny subject, you may need to employ a cast shadow at the base of the immediate foreground to enhance or accent the sunny effect beyond. You may be doing a vista in which most of the foreground must be omitted so that you can include all of the distant objects. A third composition may be from a hill, looking down at the subject with the foreground eliminated entirely.

It is only when you have been painting for quite some time that you will begin to realize that your compositions seem to lack impact—that they are too ordinary. That is when you will start to break all the so-called rules of composition and think in terms of design. Then you can distort shapes, transpose light and shade, invent forms, and be on your way toward being a creative artist.

The Horizontal versus the Vertical Composition

It is natural, in our way of seeing subjects, to view them automatically as horizontal compositions. Ever since the early days of mural painting, in which historic events were

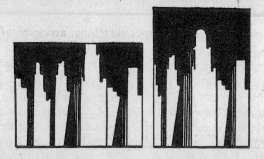

depicted, the horizontal shape has proved to be the most flexible. And as more action can take place on a horizontal plane, stage-settings and motion pictures have contributed to this way of seeing. Witness today's wider movie screen.

As you continue to work on panels that fit a 12-x-16-inch paint box, you become used to composing your subjects in that proportion. The panels set so conveniently in the horizontal lid lead to the overlooking of many subjects that would have greater impact in a vertical composition, and frequently the habit becomes so fixed that even when a student works at an easel he automatically fastens the canvas in a horizontal position before he starts to work.

If upright lines predominate in a subject, the composition will be more easily arrived at if a vertical canvas is used. Typical, if obvious, subjects would be churches and skyscrapers. A vertical shape immediately imparts a majestic feeling to your painting.

Use the view-finder described on page 80 to help you plan the shape of your composition. Later in your painting career, when you are breaking all the rules of basic composition, you will go through the stage of using thin, elongated or extremely shallow canvases that will be a challenge to compose.

Awkward Alignment

Occasionally, in on-the-spot sketching, awkward align-

ments occur. The sketches above are typical of the sort of thing that should be guarded against in making a composition.

Composition A shows the line of the dock even with the horizon. Lowering the horizon line a trifle would break this continuous, awkward line.

Composition B illustrates a situation in which the tree seems to be growing from the man's head! Moving the figure to one side of the tree would improve the arrangement.

Composition C illustrates an alignment that appears in the paintings of many students. The vertical line of the distant church is a continuation of the upright line of the shed. A more pleasing composition would result if the church were placed a bit to the left.

Composition D is an example of alignment that does not happen often in on-the-spot sketches, but does appear in studio-contrived pictures. The chances of painting a moving object, such as the sail of the boat, to line up with the cliff are extremely remote when working directly from nature. It is generally when such a composition is worked on in the studio that this continuing line occurs.

Placing a Head on the Canvas

A proven device for the placing of a head on a canvas is the "envelope fold" method. Two diagonal lines are drawn from opposite corners across the canvas. A pleasing arrangement is arrived at by placing the base of the chin where the diagonal lines cross, as illustrated.

THIS OR THIS RATHER THAN THIS

Placing the Horizon Line

While important paintings have been created with the horizon line in the middle of the canvas, it is generally better to place the horizon above or below the center, to avoid monotony.

Avoiding Horizontal Lines

Too many horizontal lines create a feeling of monotony and make the subject unexciting. Below, on the left, is an example of an uninteresting series of horizontal lines that make the subject appear dull.

By destroying as many of the horizontal lines as possible and accenting the angular aspect, the subject is immediately made more interesting. Notice how the composition on the right is improved by a downward sweep of the cloud formation. Only part of the foreground appears, and the horizontal line of the distant shoreline is broken by the sailboat.

The Vital Darks

It is the placing of the dark areas in a composition that will decide whether the picture is exciting or dull.

Thumbnail Notes

Make it a habit to do several small pencil compositions of the subject before you start to paint (see Harbor Vista, page 118). They do not have to be finished or polished drawings—indeed, they can be very fragmentary. The important point is that you have at least felt around for the best composition of the subject. It is possible that you will select the first sketch as the best, but you will have the satisfaction of knowing that you tried to exhaust the possibilities of the subject.

Rearranging Elements

As you progress you will feel the need of rearranging elements in the scene before you to improve the composition. Do not hesitate to do so. Moving a tree in the background so that it frames or accents an object of interest in the foreground will often result in a better composition. Eliminate unsightly objects. Any adjustment that will aid in producing a better picture should be made. It is through the process of rearranging and eliminating that monotony is avoided.

Painting a Complicated Subject

When attempting to paint a rather complicated subject, first make a very detailed drawing on your canvas. Such preparation will help to clarify the problem. Do not be concerned if your drawing becomes too tight; as you paint you can eliminate the unnecessary details.

SAME COLOR GUIDES EYE

Repeating Elements to Guide the Eye

The spectator's eye is guided by the repetition of both shapes and colors in a painting. These elements must vary in size and should be arranged interestingly to avoid monotony.

The Emotional Aspect of Line

The basic use of line is illustrated above.

Arranging Line to Guide the Eye

The spectator's eye is controlled by the painter's use of line. An extreme example would be a road starting at the base of the picture and leading the eye along until it arrives at the center of interest. It would make this device even more obvious if a figure were walking along the road toward the center of interest. Try to make your own compositions more subtle, but a definite arrangement must be arrived at to guide and hold the viewer's eye.

Space in a Composition

The amount of space which surrounds the objects in your composition is most important. The subject can be dwarfed by too much space, or it may give the feeling of being "hemmed in" if there is too little.

Convex and Concave Lines

Keep your lines as convex as possible to suggest strength and solidity. Concave lines weaken the structure.

White and Black

When making your thumbnail black-and-white compositions, experiment with reversing the ingredients. Using black paper and white paint will make you more conscious of the space around the objects, and a more simple, poster-like effect will result. You will also realize the importance of the shape areas behind the object.

Avoid Objects of Equal Size in the Vital Area

Do not have two objects of equal size occupying the main area of your canvas. One must be chosen to be the center of interest and the other subordinated to it.

Division of Space

Another monotonous division of space to be avoided is a diagonal line dividing the composition into two equal parts, as shown above.

The Decorative Vignette

The vignette is thought of as being primarily a decorative picture, but it is also an excellent way to practice simplified design. The vignetted edges may look casual in the finished picture, but they require planning.

Concentrating on the Center of Interest

Once you decide what is to be the center of interest in your painting make everything else subordinate to it. It may be necessary to reduce some of the secondary color areas or to modify some of the surrounding shapes. Every device possible should be used to lead the viewer to the main center of interest and to play down any disconcerting elements.

Simplifying the Subject

The student often reaches the stage at which he includes many unnecessary details. This is permissible when doing a study of a subject for future reference. However, in the development of his studio painting from detailed studies the student often becomes over-elaborate. A good exercise is to sketch from nature, reducing the scene before you to a poster-like picture. Simplify as much as possible, reducing the various color tones to single flat colors. Do a series of such sketches, using the same motif. Each time you do a new one try to make it simpler than the last.

Textural Effects for Added Interest

While the art world is going through a "textural effects" phase, do not allow yourself to become obsessed with creating textured surfaces for their own sake. Students too frequently concentrate on the surface effect and the more important elements of design and drawing suffer. Textural effects should be considered, but only in so far as they *add* interest to the overall arrangement of the shapes, color, and tone.

Adding Importance to the Center of Interest

Planning your composition with a very low eye-level perspective will make the center of interest loom up majestically. This arrangement is particularly effective in pictures depicting churches, monuments, public buildings, etc.

The Relation of One Object to Another

After the main theme has been decided upon, the relative importance of each object that makes up the scene before you should be considered before it is painted.

CASEIN-PAINTING DEMONSTRATIONS

Western Vista

The color plates on the opposite page show the start of a casein painting (see page 173) and the finished work.

I have chosen a grayish-green paper to work on to demonstrate the tremendous covering power of casein color. Although a similar effect could be obtained by using water colors mixed to an opaque consistency with white paint, the finished painting would lack the intensity of color.

Casein is also more flexible. You can start a painting using casein diluted as you would regular water colors, then, by using less water and more casein, attain an opaque effect.

The first stage of Western Vista illustrates this approach. After the pencil drawing is completed, casein color is applied over the foreground and middle distance. The sky and the distant area are untouched, revealing the grayish-green paper.

Plenty of water is used in the initial effort, resulting in a transparent effect. Then the amount of water is gradually cut down to just enough to make the casein workable, and the painting now acquires an opaque quality. However, any of the transparent areas that help achieve effective passages of color are left untouched.

Using this same approach, combining transparent and opaque techniques, the entire paper is covered until the painting is completed.

The colors I used for this casein painting and the one on the following pages were Alizarin Crimson, Burnt Umber, Cadmium Yellow Light, Cobalt Blue, Indian Red, Thalo Green, Yellow Ochre, Ivory Black, and Titan White.

The preliminary lay-in of casein color is started. The background is still untouched, revealing the original gray-toned surface of the paper.

The completed casein painting.

Seagull Cove

Seagull Cove is an example of using casein in a manner similar to an oil painter's approach to the subject. A rough penciled indication is made of the composition. This is followed by strengthening the drawing of the subject with a brush, using French Ultramarine. With the same color, the water area is quickly painted in as shown in the plate below. Then, with Burnt Umber, the cliff on the left side and the house and foreground are painted in monochromatic values. The pattern of the picture immediately takes form when these areas are covered.

This is followed by painting the shore and the cliffs in the middle ground. All this is done in a loose manner, similar to a lay-in of an oil painting. The color plate at the top of the opposite page shows the painting at this stage.

The painting continues with the modeling of the various forms, the refinement of the color, and the addition of necessary details until the subject is complete.

You may want to experiment in obtaining an oil effect by varnishing a casein painting. Use special casein varnish, perhaps several coats to give a high gloss. Place the painting in a heavy frame, omitting a mat, and it will resemble an oil painting.

French Ultramarine is used to outline the subject. Then, using the same color, the water area is painted.

The rest of the surface is quickly covered in a loose manner as shown above.

The finished painting.

The casein underpainting.

Finished with oil paint and glazes

TECHNICAL INFORMATION

TECHNICAL TIPS

Moth Balls for Sable Brushes

If you purchase expensive sable brushes for future use, put them in a tightly closed box or envelope, but not before you place a few moth balls or some similar repellent in the container. Moths love sable.

Framing an Oil Painting with Glass

At one time it was considered both fashionable and good protection to use glass when framing an oil painting, but it is seldom done today. If you should have occasion to use glass, make certain that it does not touch the surface of the painting. Small chips of wood or cork can be glued at intervals along the edge of the glass corners facing the painting, and the picture will then rest against the chips and not touch the glass. In a small painting, chips will be needed only in the four corners. Make certain that the chips are small enough so that they do not extend beyond the rabbet of the frame.

Indelible Drawing Pencils

Never use an indelible pencil or a similar marking implement for doing preliminary drawing on the canvas. The indelible dye will come through the subsequent layer of paint. If you use a board, such as Presdwood or Masonite, as a painting surface, make certain that you do not use a piece with identification marking stamped on it. Chances are an indelible ink pad was used. Never use carbon paper when transferring a drawing to canvas or to water-color paper.

Keeping Water Colors Moist

A small piece of wet sponge in the corner of your water-color box will help keep the paints moist when not in use. However, in a damp climate mold will set in after a short time.

Storing Water-Color Paper

Store your reserve supply of water-color paper in a dry place. Dampness will affect the surface, causing blotches to appear when a color wash is laid over the paper. Take care, when unpacking unused water-color paper, not to rub one sheet against another, for the surface bruises easily. Avoid unnecessary handling—a grease mark made by the fingers will produce a blemish when paint is applied.

Affixing Paper to a Rigid Base

Use pure white library paste when affixing paper to cardboard, because rubber cement or glue will eventually work through and stain the paper. Never apply pressure directly; instead, place a sheet of bond paper or clean wrapping paper over the surface being mounted. Then use the heel of your hand or a roller, applying the pressure from the center to the edges.

Wax Finish for Paintings

Oil and casein paintings can be given a wax coating after being varnished. A casein painting on a gesso panel especially can often be enhanced by wax. Casein varnish is first applied to the panel, bringing out all the color possible, and the resulting shine is often objectionable to many painters, who tone down the varnish by applying wax with a soft, lintless rag. The wax dulls the surface at first, but it can be gradually worked up into as much gloss as desired by rubbing with a circular motion.

Giving Your Brushes an Occasional Rest

Brushes, particularly those used for water color, become limp when used daily. Give them a good washing with a mild soap and rinse thoroughly in tepid to cool water (hot water can loosen the hairs). Squeeze the surplus water out and reshape the hairs. Place them brush up in a jar for a time and they will regain their spring and resiliency.

Protecting the Finish of Art Work

The plastic sprays that are on the market today can be used to protect and preserve the surface of many varieties of finished art work. These sprays are especially useful for keeping pencil and charcoal drawings from smudging, and they also provide a protective coating for poster and casein paint. However, once the surface is sprayed it is no longer workable, for paint added onto a plastic base may chip or flake off.

Flattening Rolled Paper

If you have kept your reserve supply of drawing or water-color paper rolled up, you can flatten it this way: Place the paper on a drawing board with the curve bellying toward you. Dampen the paper with a moist sponge, and pin the corners with thumb tacks. As it dries it will become flat.

Working in the Sun

When you work outdoors facing the sun, light often

shows through a stretched canvas. This can be most disconcerting at the early stage of laying-in a subject. If you have a reserve panel in your paint box place it at the back of the canvas, or tack a few sheets of newspaper on the back.

Cleaning Mats

The delicate surface of mat board bruises easily and frequently starts to peel when rubbed with an eraser. Try using a household cleansing powder with a soft rag. Sprinkle the powder lightly over the mat and rub gently with a circular motion.

Controlled Drying of a Water Color

A hand-operated hair dryer can be used to hasten the drying of a water color. The gradation of a wet wash can be varied by placing the dryer closer to the area that you wish to dry lighter and holding it there for a longer time. The faster the wet surface dries, the lighter the final tone.

Using the Reverse Side of a Spoiled Water-Color Paper

You can paint on the unused side of good-quality paper. It is advisable to clean the surface with a sponge and clear water first, to remove any grease spots that may have accumulated and thus provide a more receptive working surface.

Eliminating Bubbles on Mounted Paper

Sometimes a small, raised, bubble-like spot appears on the surface of the paper you have just mounted. Just pick this air pocket with a needle. This will release the air and the spot will disappear when pressure is applied.

Keeping Casein Soluble

Casein will stay water-soluble on a metal or plastic palette for days if a wet cloth is placed over it.

Avoiding Eyestrain

Use a tinted paper for sketching a series of subjects that must be rendered in bright sunlight. The usual white surface reflects the glare and is difficult to work on and hard on the eyes. Cream-colored detail paper has an excellent surface and is inexpensive.

Disposable Palette

There is a palette available made up of 50 sheets in a pad-like form. You squeeze out and arrange your paints in the usual way on the top sheet, and instead of cleaning up left-over paint you simply tear off the sheet.

Retarding the Drying of Water Color

A few drops of glycerine in the water before mixing water color will make the color dry more slowly.

Sketch At All Times

OIL-PAINTING TIPS

Salvaging Surplus Paint

Oil paint left on the palette can be saved by placing it in a deep dish and filling the dish with enough water to cover all the paint. When ready to use the paint again, pour off the water and transfer the colors back to your palette. Your palette knife will facilitate the handling of the paint.

Removing Dried Paint from a Palette Knife

Oil paint that has dried hard on your palette knife can be removed by dipping the knife in paint remover. A razor blade can also be used to scrape paint off, but take care not to nick the edge of the knife.

Holder for Palette Knife and Brushes

There is a clip-on gadget sold in five-and-ten-cent stores for use in the kitchen to hold knives and such equipment. It can be fastened to the side of your taboret or work table and makes a convenient place to keep your brushes and palette knife.

Storing Canvas

Do not keep your roll of canvas in a cold room. The sizing and white lead coating become brittle and are likely to crack when unrolled.

Making Your Own Textured Board

If you use a compressed-fiber board you can produce your own texture when preparing the board for painting.

After the usual sandpapering to roughen the surface, give it a coat of white lead and allow it to dry. Apply a second coat, but instead of brushing smoothly, pounce the paint with a stiff bristle brush. An old brush cut flat like a stencil brush is excellent. Unlike the ready-prepared mechanically textured boards that have a monotonously even surface, yours can have an interesting textured effect, as rough and uneven as you like. The surface can always be sanded down if certain areas are too rough.

Resurfacing an Old Canvas

You can re-use a discarded painting, but do not work directly over the old paint. First scrape the ridges of paint down to a flat surface, using your palette knife and sand-paper. Wipe thoroughly and coat it with white paint. The coating will dry faster and harder if the white lead is cut with copal oil varnish. A brush can be used, but a palette knife will give a better working surface. Apply the coating just heavily enough to cover the previous painting, and let it dry thoroughly before starting a new painting.

Improving the Surface of a Cotton Canvas Panel

The procedure for resurfacing canvas can be used on new, stretched cotton canvas. The coating is particularly good for cheap cotton panels, which are notoriously absorbent. The subsequent painting will hold its color more readily because the paint will not sink in as much when it dries.

Keeping Your Hands Clean

If you dislike the task of removing oil paint stains from your hands, there is a preparation that might interest you. It is a hand cream that is applied before you start to paint;

it forms a protective layer that is easily removed with water at the end of a work session, taking any oil stains with it.

Kerosene for Cleaning Brushes

Many painters use kerosene for cleaning oil brushes, claiming that it keeps the brush soft without affecting its spring. This is done at the end of the day's work, never while painting. Kerosene mixed with oil paint will eventually darken the color.

Eliminating Excess Oil Content

If the oil paints with which you are working have too much oil content, squeeze them out on a newspaper first. The newspaper will absorb the excess oil, and the colors can then be transferred to your palette as needed for mixing.

Preserving Your Palette

Before using a new palette, pour a little linseed oil on it. Then, using a soft, clean rag, rub oil over the entire surface and repeat this on the reverse side. Allow the oil to sink into the wood thoroughly.

Getting the Most Out of a Tube of Paint

Always squeeze the paint from the base of the tube. As the paint is used, roll up the bottom of the tube. It is surprising how much more paint can be obtained from a tube by following this simple procedure.

PAINTING A LARGE PICTURE

As you progress you will eventually want to do a larger painting than the 12-x-16- or 16-x-20-inch canvases you have probably been using to paint from nature.

Oil paintings that are being exhibited in most shows today are not as large as those displayed in the past. Average sizes today are 25 x 30, 30 x 36, and 30 x 40 inches, plus the width of the frame. Many art societies limit the over-all size because wall space is limited, and since paintings often have to be shipped, costs also help to limit the size.

I suggest that you paint your first larger canvas 25 x 30 inches. While this is not an impressive size, compared to many of the paintings you have seen exhibited, it will offer enough problems. It should be painted in the studio, using one of your most successful small on-the-spot sketches for reference.

The several ways of enlarging a sketch are described on pages 228-229. Probably the best way is to redraw it with charcoal on the large white canvas. You can reshape, add to, or eliminate any areas you like, to help the painting. It is seldom that the spot sketch can be enlarged line for line to a larger canvas and still be a satisfactory composition. You will also discover, very shortly after you begin to apply the paint, that color passages which seemed attractive in a small canvas have lost something when enlarged.

This is natural enough when you analyze the problem. On a small canvas bits of attractive color seem more exciting. Sometimes they are only shapeless daubs of the brush but they add life to the sketch. However, when you work large, these shapeless daubs and exciting bits of color must take form and be correct in tonal value. This is where the student encounters his first pitfall. There is also the problem of paint quality. A passage of painting that was pleasing in the small canvas often becomes very thin when enlarged. The edges of the different color areas have to be handled more carefully; you cannot get away with just smudging it or making it fuzzy! And last, there is the drawing. What was just a few wisps of paint and a small walking figure must now be more delineated.

All these problems will have to be solved when doing the large canvas. Use as large a brush as possible and do not be too concerned with brush work and textural quality at this stage. Follow the form of the objects with the brush as simply as possible. Try to obtain a pleasing color arrangement, but, most important, concentrate on the correct values.

You may also want to experiment with underpainting when doing a large painting in the studio. A vibrant effect is obtained by painting a warm color over an area that is to appear cooler in the final painting. For example, the sky could be painted a pinkish tone, then the blue sky color applied over the pink. You can carry such experiments further by allowing the undertone to dry thoroughly before painting over it. This produces interesting color effects and textural quality.

VARNISHING AN OIL PAINTING

Varnishing protects the finished painting from dirt and moisture and at the same time brightens the areas that have dried dull, producing an even sheen on the entire surface of the painting.

However, a final varnish should not be applied until the painting is thoroughly dry. Some paintings dry more slowly than others, so it is wise to allow a minimum of at least three months. In the meantime retouch varnish can serve as a temporary measure. This can be applied as soon as the painting is dry to the touch.

I find copal picture varnish very satisfactory for the final varnishing; it dries with a hard finish. Make certain that the painting is clean before applying the final varnish. Use a lintless cloth to remove any dust that may have accumulated in the three-month drying period. Pour a small amount of varnish into a dish, so that it is easily accessible with the brush, and use a soft housepainter's brush of 1-inch to 1½-inch width.

Place the painting in a horizontal position and varnish as uniformly as possible, overlapping each stroke slightly to make certain that all of it is varnished. Leave the painting in a horizontal position until dry, otherwise the varnish will run. For an added gloss you can repeat the above process on the following day.

Varnish can also be applied with a spray. Special cans are available which have built-in atomizers for spraying the varnish evenly.

Avoid varnishing a painting on a damp day, because the drying will be considerably retarded.

GLAZING AND SCUMBLING

Glazing and scumbling are methods of enhancing or modifying a painting.

A glaze is an oil color reduced to a watery, transparent consistency and applied with a soft brush over a direct area. It imparts more depth and luminosity to the area. The area should be on the light side, for a glaze intensifies and darkens the section it covers.

You can use copal painting medium to reduce oil color to a glazing consistency. If it is still too heavy add some turpentine to thin it. There are media made expressly for glazing—a preparation called Gel is very good. It will reduce any oil color to the desired transparency and requires no turpentine or oil.

Glazing is most successful when done gradually in successive applications. Drying time must be allowed for each glaze.

Experiment by superimposing warm and cool color glazes. You can glaze part of a painting or all of it, but make sure that the surface you are working on is thoroughly dry.

Scumbling is generally used to lighten a dried area. The paint is applied as it comes from the tube and is mixed to the desired color. Medium is seldom used, for there is enough oil content in the paint to make it workable. The paint is dragged over the dried area, producing a broken effect of color and an interesting textural quality as well. It is also useful in softening any harsh color or details.

Experiment on a discarded canvas, by scumbling over various areas, reducing tones, creating textural effects, enhancing color, and so on.

OPAQUE AND TRANSPARENT QUALITIES
IN OIL COLORS

Oil colors vary in their degree of transparency. You will soon discover how much more the transparent colors on your palette are affected than the opaque colors, when mixed with white.

This does not necessarily mean that all transparent colors possess less tinting strength. On the contrary, such transparent and semi-transparent colors as Prussian Blue, Thalo Green, Thalo Blue, and Alizarin Crimson have a powerful tinting capacity.

It is useful to know of this varying degree of transparency in the colors on your palette, both for mixing and for glazing and scumbling.

Opaque

Burnt Umber
Cadmium colors (all)
Cerulean Blue
Chromium Oxide Green (opaque)
Indian Red
Light Red
Mars colors (all)
Naples Yellow
Raw Umber
Vermilion
Whites (all)

Semi-Opaque

Lamp Black
Lemon Yellow (Hansa Yellow)
Permanent Green, Light
Terra Rosa
Yellow Ochre
Zinc Yellow

Semi-Transparent

Brown Madder
Cobalt Blue
Gold Ochre
Ivory Black
Payne's Gray
Permanent Green, Deep
Prussian Blue
Raw Sienna
Thalo Blue
Thalo Green
Thalo Red Rose
Thalo Yellow Green

Transparent

Alizarin Crimson
Burnt Sienna
Green Earth
Permanent Blue
Rose Madder
Ultramarines (all)
Viridian

DRYING TIME OF VARIOUS OIL COLORS

It is useful to know just which colors are fast-drying and which dry slowly. For example, a fast-drying color is especially needed in the preliminary lay-in of color, when you want the underpainting to dry as quickly and thoroughly as possible before you resume painting. At other times you may want the colors to remain as workable as possible from day to day, and may find a palette of slow-drying colors desirable. This is important in portrait work, when you want to keep the paint flexible enough for successive sittings to complete the modeling of the head and features. Of course, retarders or driers can be added to control the paint, but they should be used sparingly. Keep in mind that the thickness of the paint and the atmospheric conditions at the time affect drying time.

Fast

Burnt Umber	*Prussian Blue*
Cobalt Blue	*Raw Umber*
Payne's Gray	*Viridian*

Medium

Burnt Sienna	*Light Red*
Chromium Oxide Green	*Naples Yellow*
French Ultramarine	*Thalo colors (all)*
Hansa colors (all)	*Yellow Ochre*

Slow

Alizarin Crimson	*Cadmium Yellow*
Cadmium Orange	*Zinc White*
Cadmium Red	

THE CARE OF YOUR PICTURES

The use of retouch varnish as a temporary protection until a final varnish can be applied has already been discussed (see page 221).

Care must also be taken to protect the back of the canvas, particularly when sending the painting to an exhibition. There is always the danger of a dent or a hole being made in a canvas when several are stacked together. This can happen in your studio as easily as when they arrive at an exhibition. A piece of strong heavy cardboard, cut to the size of the painting and tacked to the wooden canvas strips, will minimize this danger.

If a painting is damaged by a tear or a hole accidentally poked through a vital spot, it can be repaired by re-backing the canvas. To start, the canvas must be perfectly dry. Remove the tacks and separate the canvas from its stretchers. Cut a piece of new canvas with a margin (including the tacking area) about an inch larger than the damaged canvas. Place the fresh canvas right side up on the floor and spread a heavy layer of white lead, cut with linseed oil, evenly over all of it. Now place the back side of the damaged canvas against the new canvas and apply even pressure over the entire area. Any surplus white lead that oozes out will be deposited on the 1-inch margin of the fresh canvas and can easily be scraped off. Put a sheet of waxed paper cut to the size of the damaged painting over the face of the painting and place everything under a flat drawing board. Let it dry for several days. Remove the board, trim the margin, and restretch. It is not always necessary to re-back or reline the entire canvas. For a small tear, a patch made from new canvas can be applied. Whether the painting is patched or re-backed, some retouching will be necessary if the hole or tear is of any size.

Oil paintings that have been stored for some time in a closet or on a curtained rack may darken or yellow. They will brighten considerably if you place them where they will be exposed to constant daylight (not direct sunlight). Keep this in mind if you are planning to exhibit any older paintings, so that they will be shown to best advantage. It is also possible that a new coating of varnish will help; some dull spots may have developed because of color sinking into the canvas.

It is good practice to keep a case history of paintings that are the result of experimentation. This experimentation can be the paints used for an underpainting, new colors that you have added to your palette, time allowed for paint layers to dry, or any new approach. This information can be written on the back of the stretcher strips and will often provide vital data for future paintings.

Your water colors will give you less of a preservation problem than your oil paintings. They can be stored in portfolios with hinged flaps to keep out the dust and placed in a horizontal position to prevent warping.

A water color that has been soiled by dirt or dust can be cleaned with a kneaded eraser. Bread crumbs can also be used as a gentle means of removing accumulated dust smears. If a water color has a crease in it, moisten the back with clear water on a sponge. Then rub the under side of a spoon gently over the crease to help smooth it. Put the sheet between two clean blotters and place it under a drawing board, using some books for added pressure. Allow it to press for a few days before rematting.

METHODS OF ENLARGING AND TRANSFERRING
SKETCHES AND DRAWINGS

In Painting a Large Picture, page 219, reference was made to enlarging a sketch as a base for a larger canvas.

There are several ways of enlarging a sketch or a drawing. The simplest method is "squaring up" the sketch and transferring the composition to a canvas or a sheet of watercolor paper.

If the sketch is 8 x 10 inches it is divided into 2-inch, pencil-ruled squares. Assuming that it is to be enlarged to twice its size, that is, to 16 x 20 inches, 4-inch squares are drawn on the blank canvas.

The squares act as a guide for each area of the composition and it is a simple matter to fill in each of them. This enlarging method can be used for a picture of any size. If the subject is complex, you may want to use more and smaller squares; on the other hand, a simple subject may require only a few squares. Any incidental passages of intricate drawing that occur can be subdivided as illustrated.

If you want to keep the sketch intact, place a sheet of transparent paper or glass over it. The squaring-up process can then be done on the protective sheet without harm to the original. Use a grease or china marking pencil on glass, to make sure the lines will show, and use a soft pencil on the transparent paper so that the ruled lines will not indent the sketch. Charcoal can be used on the canvas for the enlarged drawing.

There are several mechanical devices that can be used for enlarging, such as the pantograph, proportional dividers, and others, but you will find the squaring-up method convenient for most subjects.

You may some time have a sketch photostated and enlarged to the desired size, then trace the photostat on the canvas. This is an inexpensive way of copying material and making it any size. First rub the back of the photostatic copy with graphite or charcoal, then thumb-tack it to the canvas and trace through, using a hard pencil. The traced image can be sprayed with a fixatif or redrawn directly with a brush and thinned oil color.

At the left is the sketch that has been squared for enlarging.

Below are the corresponding squares enlarged on the canvas and ready for painting.

FRAMING OIL PAINTINGS

Many amateurs spend valuable time painting their subject and buy the best quality of paints and equipment—then they place their efforts in a cheap thin five-and-ten-cent-store frame. Even a professionally executed painting would not look very impressive in such a setting.

I admit that no amount of money spent on a frame will improve the painting as a work of art, but a tastefully selected frame will certainly improve its over-all appearance.

You can purchase suitable molding from a lumber yard and, using a miter saw, make your own frames, but this is time-consuming. Rather, compromise and buy the raw wood frames that are now sold in all art supply shops and many department stores. The sizes that fit stock-size canvases are very reasonable in price. Just make certain that the frame you select is heavy enough in width for your painting.

You should apply some type of finish to the raw wood, even if only a flat gray tone. Putting a finish on the raw frame can be fascinating work and can be done at a time when you have become "stale" and lack desire or inspiration to paint. All artists go through such periods, especially after a season's work or a one-man show, and many take advantage of these times by finishing frames, cutting mats, and reading about art and artists.

MATTING AND FRAMING WATER COLORS

At one time all water colors were displayed in mats of generous margins, and it is still difficult to surpass the enhancing effect of a wide white mat on a simply framed transparent water color. Nowadays, however, when water colors are painted in larger sizes and are heavier in both color and paint content, many artists exhibit their paintings in wide, carved frames with very narrow mats. In some cases the mat is eliminated and an inset is used instead. The method you use is a matter of personal preference, and the key in which you work should help determine the choice. A wide frame with just an inset would certainly look too heavy for a high-keyed water color.

Have on hand mats with various-sized openings to place over your sketches when you return to the studio. Their appearance is immediately improved, and it is easier to judge the over-all effect with the mat providing a clean, sharp edge.

A mat is also helpful when working indoors on a water color. Placing the picture in the mat as you near the final stages helps in determining how much more work is needed. You will often be pleasantly surprised at how little work is left when your painting is viewed this way. Never display water colors to anyone without a mat, in fairness to him as well as to yourself, because it is difficult to judge an unmatted painting. At the final stage it is also wise to place glass over the water color, for the smooth sheen always adds depth as well as finish to a painting.

FRAMING

The detailed or "busy" subject is displayed best in a simple frame.

A more ornate frame enhances the simple subject.

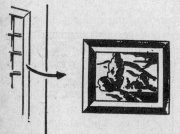

The picture will appear to its best advantage when the light from the window or lamp that illuminates it comes from the same direction as the light in the painting.

MATTING

The rectangular mat has the widest margin at the base. The margins of the sides and top are of equal width.

The vertical mat has, generally, the same mat margins as the rectangular mat. However, many liberties can be taken in varying the margins, especially when the picture is extremely elongated.

A wide mat with colored lines that harmonize with the subject gives a pleasing over-all effect.

FINISHING YOUR OWN FRAMES

Following are recipes for putting various finishes on raw wood frames. They are not too time-consuming and will definitely enhance the presentation of your paintings. Just make certain that the width of the frame itself is heavy enough for your painting.

• For a simple water-color frame a coat of white shellac will suffice for a quick job. Make certain that the raw wood is well sandpapered and that the surface is clean before the shellac is applied. When dry, rub down with fine steel wool.

• Maple, walnut, mahogany, and other stains can be used. Select a shade that harmonizes with the water-color and apply to a clean sandpapered surface. Rub down lightly with steel wool when dry. A paste wax can be used to give a protective finish and a slight gloss.

• Casein paint is excellent for obtaining a quick finish for narrow or heavy frames. A warm gray is produced by mixing white and a touch of raw umber in casein colors. Applied directly to the raw wood, in a heavy consistency, it can be textured before it dries. An effective ridged texture can be obtained with an ordinary comb. You can also produce a stippled effect by pounding the wet casein surface with a stiff stencil brush. Old toothbrushes, shaving brushes, and the like also make handy texturing implements.

• Second-hand gold frames can be used to excellent advantage after they have been pleasingly toned. Brush a casein mixture over the gold and allow it to dry. Then, using a fine sandpaper, rub it down, allowing parts of the original gold to show through.

FRAMING TIPS

• Rubber or cork tips placed in the lower corners of the back of a frame will keep the picture from tilting and will also prevent the wall from becoming streaked.

• If you keep your paintings a standard size, you can use inexpensive stock frames. These are obtainable in many designs, and give you the added advantage of being able to try several types of frames for the same painting.

• A small piece of cellulose tape placed on the wall before the supporting nail or hook is driven in will prevent the plaster from chipping.

• Keep several mats of various colors on hand. It is surprising how a warm gray mat will enhance the appearance of a certain water color in contrast to the usual white. Even a slightly off-white tone may be a vast improvement over a dead-white mat.

• You can put button backs on water-color frames to eliminate nails. The big advantage, however, is that the pictures can be changed easily.

• Dip your glass cutter into some turpentine before cutting a piece of glass for a frame—it will cut much easier.

• To keep your picture flat against the wall, place the picture rings as near the top of the frame as possible. When it is necessary to have the picture tilt forward, to eliminate reflections, for instance, place the rings lower.

EXHIBITING PAINTINGS

Almost every painter arrives at the stage when he would like to exhibit his work. I think that it is a good idea to have your paintings shown with those of others; it gives you a fresh perspective on your work, because it is surprising how different your picture looks on a wall surrounded by paintings of other artists. Sometimes you are agreeably surprised when your painting holds its own in comparison. At other times the painting that seemed so colorful and strong in your studio looks drab and weak alongside the other pictures.

If your work looks disappointing, you may first be inclined to blame the lighting, the other artists' frames, or the place where the hanging committee placed your painting. Any or all of these reasons may be the right ones, but it is quite possible that the painting itself is to blame!

If you exhibit too soon in your career you are bound to be disappointed. Rather, attend various exhibitions, carefully observing all the paintings on display. Then, when you feel that your work is comparable to that of the exhibiting artists, submit your paintings. I use the word "submit" because I am thinking in terms of open exhibits that are juried.

It may be more feasible for you to join a local art group or club. These groups have exhibitions for their members, and such exhibitions, besides being stimulating, can be stepping stones to competitive juried shows.

However you chose to exhibit your work, keep foremost in your mind that you are painting to satisfy yourself rather than a jury.

GLOSSARY OF ART TERMS

Accent The emphasis of dark or light in a drawing, or of color in a painting.

Alla Prima A method by which a painting is usually completed in one sitting—painting in a direct manner.

Aniline A derivative of coal tar used to produce brilliant, but not necessarily permanent, colors.

Blend To merge together or soften.

Bright A brush with short-haired bristles.

Broken Color Color that is broken by another color.

Cast Shadow The shadow that is cast from one form onto another.

Classical Established ideals of perfection.

Coat A layer of paint.

Chroma The element in color that indicates its degree of saturation.

Design The planned composition of a work of art.

Fat Rich in oil content.

Ferrule	The metal band encircling a brush and holding the hairs.
Fixatif	A thin varnish of watery consistency, used to keep drawings from smudging.
Flat	A brush with long-haired bristles.
Flat Color	An even or uniform area of color.
Genre	A type of realistic, story-telling painting.
Gesso	A plasterlike material spread upon a surface to prepare it for painting.
Glaze	Transparent painting over a light underpainting.
Gouache	1. A painting with opaque or body colors. 2. Non-transparent.
Graduated Color	The range of color from light to dark or from warm to cool that results in a gradually changing effect.
Grisaille	The painting of the subject in gray colors, used as an underpainting.
Impasto	1. Thick application of pigment. 2. The pigment so applied.
Mat	The surrounding area between the frame and the picture.
Matte	A dull surface.

Medium	1. The means of drawing or painting— oil, water color, pen and ink, and so on are media. 2. The binder for the pigments, the vehicle.
Monochrome	A painting executed with one color.
Motif	The theme or source.
Muted Color	Restricted or suppressed rather than the full range of color.
Neutral Color	A color without definite identification.
Nocturne	A night scene.
Opaque	Heavy or non-transparent.
Palette	1. A rectangular- or oval-shaped flat surface used for mixing colors. 2. The selection of colors used by an artist.
Prime	To make ready. The preparatory coating.
Rabbet	The recess or groove of a frame for holding the picture.
Reflected Light	The shadowed part of an object which is lightened by the reflection from an adjacent object.
Saturation	The greatest possible intensity of the color.

Scumbling	Dragging paint in a broken manner over a previously painted dry surface.
Sketch	1. A brief statement of the subject. 2. A drawing complete in itself.
Study	1. A comprehensive drawing or painting. 2. A detail that can be incorporated into a finished painting.
Stretcher	The wooden frame on which canvas or paper is stretched.
Support	The surface material on which the paint is applied.
Tacky	Sticky, partly dried.
Tint	A light hue of color.
Tooth	The textural surface quality of the white canvas, varying from rough to smooth.
Tone	The changes of color achieved by lightening with white or darkening with black.
Value	The difference in effect due to light and dark.
Wash	1. The application of color in a thin, fluid manner. 2. Diluted pigment.